PRAISE FOR:

DO IT WITH YOUR SHOES ON

& 101 OTHER FUN WAYS TO SPICE UP YOUR SEX LIFE

"America, wake up and listen to what David Abels has to say about sex! Filled with funny and practical suggestions that can create big changes in your sex life, this book is sure to find its place next to the best of sex mannuals."
—Judith Seifer, Ph.D., R.N., President Elect of the American Association of Sex Educators, Counselors, and Therapists

"One of the most exciting and usable books on enhancing your sex life that I've seen in a long, long time. This book gives couples workable information with a touch of humor at a time when people seem to have forgotten that sex is supposed to be fun."
—Lavada Blanton, Penthouse Magazine

"A funny, sexy, healthy, and imaginative collection of legitimate ways to spice up your sex life. If every couple in America reads this book, no one will go to work!"
—Asa Baber, Playboy Magazine

"A remarkable collection of genuine knock-your-socks-off sex tips. Try just one or two of the fun suggestions in this book to rejuvenate your sex life."
—Beth Howard, SELF Magazine

"Lovers seeking ideas for sexual fun will find lots of sexy ideas in this book. A positive, healthy, and classy contribution to our sex-negative society."
—Roger Libby, Ph.D., Board Certified Sex Therapist and Author

"A hilariously enlightening guide to lovemaking that captures the essence of one of life's biggest secrets — sex is meant to be fun! Buy this book for anyone you really care about and tell them to do it with their shoes on!"
—Adam Glickman, President, CONDOMania

Do It With Your Shoes On

Shoes On

& 101 OTHER FUN WAYS
TO SPICE UP YOUR SEX LIFE

BY DAVID ABELS

THREE CAT PRESS
Miami Beach, Florida

BOOKS FOR THE WAY
WE LIVE, WORK, AND PLAY

Post Office Box 415106
Miami Beach, FL 33141-5106
U.S.A.
Telephone: (305) 867-1060 / (800) BOOKS-101

International Standard Book Number: 1-884477-25-9
Library of Congress Catalog Card Number: 93-95051
First Edition, First Printing, 1994

For Tannis,
my lover, my wife

License my roving hands, and let them go
Before, behind, above, below.

John Donne
English poet
(1572-1631)

TABLE OF CONTENTS

TABLE OF CONTENTS

INTRODUCTION

When it comes to your sex life, how many times have you said to yourself, "There's got to be more to this!"

You're not the only one. Even the most sexually adventurous lovers experience lulls in their lust lives that leave them wondering.

The cure, of course, is imagination. What has become boring, even tedious, can be quickly turned into fun and excitement with a little ingenuity. This book will give you 102 ways to do that.

From doing it with your shoes on to doing it by candlelight, your sex life can be drastically improved with just a few of the suggestions in this book. Try as many as you're comfortable with or alter them to fit both your needs.

We live in an era when lovemaking is taking a hard rap. In the midst of the deadly serious AIDS crisis, we all need to be cautious when it comes to sex.

But that does not mean there's no room left for fun in the sack. Practice protective sex always and avoid putting you and your lover at risk. If you've done that, there's no reason not to still have fun.

For singles, that may mean paying more attention to the lover you're with instead of shopping around, and this book will help you to do that. For married and long-term couples, putting more eroticism and seduction into your sexual lives will keep you both from straying into situations neither of you want. This book is sort of old-fashioned that way.

Beyond that, this book will remind you that you should always make your lover feel wanted, and paying attention to a lover who's bored is a way to show you care about your relationship.

In that sense, this book is addressed to all lovers. While even in the most traditional of relationships women have been the partners who tended to matters of the heart, more and more men are realizing that they need to play a part, too.

So, go ahead and enjoy this book; it's meant to be fun to read. Each of the 102 sections presents a different way to have sex that you may or may not have thought of. Read the book with your lover; it's a nice way to find out about each other and about each other's sexual desires.

My best wishes to you for a sex life where the fun never ends.

With my shoes on,

David Abels
Publisher
THREE CAT PRESS

DO IT WITH YOUR SHOES ON

& 101 OTHER FUN WAYS TO SPICE UP YOUR SEX LIFE

EDITOR'S NOTE

When I was in college, I dated the same man for three years. After two years of what we both agreed were some very good times, he shyly asked me one evening to leave on the black patent leather spike heeled shoes I was wearing while we got into bed. His request completely changed our lives.

It turned out we both had lots of fantasies we'd been dying to act out, but had been too shy to tell each other about them. Once the cat was out of the bag, so to speak, we both felt free to speak up.

A year later when we both graduated and went our separate ways, I think the reason we parted was that we were both suffering from sexual burnout. It certainly wasn't boredom.

The point is that everybody is full of ideas about what they'd like to do with, to, and for their lover, but they don't always know how or where to start. You hold in your hands the ideal solution to that little problem.

After you look through this book, pick the page that intrigues you the most. Then slip upstairs after dinner, maybe while your lover is watching the TV news, and leave the book on their pillow, open to the part you like best. While they're reading, surprise them by doing. You can blame it all on David.

But I don't think you'll have to make any excuses. You'll be amazed at how much excitement just a little change can stir up.

In fact, I still have that pair of black spiked heels. The first time I wore them to bed with my current beau, he was really turned on. Thank heavens I'm older now and have the stamina to keep up with the other desires this book has inspired!

Heels in hand,

Beth Adelman

Beth Adelman
Editor-in-Chief
THREE CAT PRESS

DO IT WITH YOUR SHOES ON

& 101 OTHER FUN WAYS TO SPICE UP YOUR SEX LIFE

1

WITH YOUR SHOES ON

Whether it's in sneakers, leather boots, penny loafers, or high heels, doing it with your shoes on can be a real turn-on. Just the sight of your lover with nothing on but their shoes may be just what you need to kick your lovemaking into high gear.

After all, what man worth his sexual weight can forget those famous *Playboy* girls posed in nothing but black heels? And what woman could turn away a Joe Montana-type standing there with just his cleats? No matter the height of the heel or the breadth of the sole, there has always been something sexy about a lover sans everything but their shoes.

Shoes are a turn-on because feet are sexy, too. There are few things like a lover's cool feet easing their way up your anatomy. Having shoes on those feet adds a little touch of the unusual, which is often what makes lovemaking fun.

Adding that touch of the unusual is easy — as easy as putting your lover's shoes on or taking them off. If you don't get the picture, maybe it's time for a trip with your lover to their favorite shoe store. Ask the salesman if you can do his dirty work, but don't let on what you're thinking. You might just get that loafer of a lover all pumped up.

2

IN THE CAR

ver since Henry Ford started turning out all those little private rooms with wheels and motors he called Model-T's, doing it in the car has been a staple of lovemakers around the world. From the supremely illicit to the innocently young, doing it in the car sets the lovemaking gears in motion.

Lovemaking in a car has all the sensuous touches of a B movie gone good — the sticky upholstery, the cold steering

wheel, the cramped quarters, and the ever-present threat of someone inducing coitus interruptus. If you or your lover have never made it with the key in the ignition, jump in the station wagon and head for the nearest deserted street or alley.

Car fetishists wouldn't have it any other way. While there's still something to be said for doing it royally in the most quiet and comfortable of surroundings, such as in the luxury of an expensive hotel, there's not much that measures up to the fun and excitement of doing it in the back seat of an old Chevrolet.

The best way to make love on wheels is in your favorite wheeled vehicle, and that can be anything from a tiny sports car to a fully stocked RV. Whatever the model and whatever its horsepower, lovemaking in a car can get your blood hot and circulating like a fuel-injected engine revving with steam.

3

ALL DRESSED UP

While some may prefer it in the buff, and others in the special costumes of their private fantasies, making it in your best duds remains a traditional favorite. In a tuxedo or an evening dress, a mate dressed to kill is as irresistible as a stack of hundred dollar bills.

Formal attire makes everything but romance seem like a waste of time; just ask Ginger Rogers, Fred Astaire, or Cary Grant. In white tie and tails or in diamonds and lace, anyone dressed to the T is hard to turn down. Even a simple but elegant tie or scarf can be the extra touch that makes making love the only thing to do. Add a low-cut cocktail dress or an Italian double breasted suit to your wardrobe and you may have your lover soon wearing nothing but a smile.

When it comes to lovemaking all dressed up, don't be afraid to pop a few buttons or tear a few seams. For the few pennies you pay the tailor to fix a hem or zipper, the excitement you'll have shared will certainly be worth the wear and tear.

Remember, too, that when you're wearing your Sunday best, always disregard whatever care labels your special clothes bear. Because the more wrinkled and stained you get your special attire, the more fun you're likely to have had.

4

WHEN THE KIDS ARE GONE

No matter how much you love your children, there are times when you wish you didn't have them. Even those who don't have kids know the feeling of having a crowded house with nowhere to go for a bit of intimacy. Whether they're your own little angels or not, kids have a habit of getting in the way of an amorous way.

There's an easy solution — get rid of them. No, not permanently, just long enough to do what you want to do. Send the younger kids to the movies, even if you have to postpone your lovemaking session to chauffeur them to the theater. For older kids, suggest a fun outing at a local fast food restaurant or the neighborhood arcade, and then send them packing as quickly as you can hand them a ten spot.

If that doesn't work, try a little white lie. Tell them the house is a mess, you're in a bad mood, and you want them to go clean their room or to go play outside. What kid would stay in the house after that?

When no one is left at home but you and your lover, the freedom and urgency of the moment will work their own magic. Be sure that in all the frenzy someone keeps an eye on the clock. When the front door opens, you may not want the kids to see you running naked through the house.

5

IN PUBLIC

Oh, for the erotic sensation of having a stranger's eyes on you and your lover in an amorous mood! From sneaking a squeeze in the elevator on the way to your office to doing it in the summer heat on a park bench, sex in public may be the stimulant that opens your lover's pores, heart, and senses.

Inside or out, having fans around to watch your loving ways may bring out the best in both of you. It's not often that everyday lovers get to do it as if they were on the big screen, and doing it in public can be as close as it comes.

Needless to say, while doing it for the masses adds excitement, it does bring its dangers. First is the chance your performance may earn you a visit to the local police station, especially if you've chosen to do it in a more foreign location than your neighbor's backyard.

Second, your performance may be so good that you draw a crowd. This can be stimulating in itself, so long as no one there gets so excited they decide to walk off with your clothes.

Of course, "public" is a relative term, and with a little care you can remain discreet and even hidden in the most pedestrian of places. The danger of imminent discovery is the naughty little secret you both can share.

6

ON THE FURNITURE

If you open yourself up to the idea that the bed is not the only place to make love, doing it with other household accouterments — such as the furniture — becomes that much more intriguing. While your old loveseat may make a nifty place for watching *Oprah*, it may make a better outpost for doing something that can actually get you on *Oprah*.

In fact, for certain types of lovemaking and the positions they require, the shapes and sizes of furniture other than your mattress might become the preferred terrain. In cases where one of you is sitting or bending over, the extra support for your hands and body that a good couch, chair or loveseat provides comes in handy.

Even the dining room table may provide an interesting love environ. If you've ever seen Jack Nicholson ring Jessica Lange's bell on that wooden table in *The Postman Always Rings Twice,* your second thoughts of doing it amidst the dinner plates may quickly disappear.

You can also try using your bed as a piece of furniture with a variety of surfaces. Who says lovemaking must be done on top of the bed? Why not holding on to the headboard? In all this new and exciting motion, you may just find a new arrangement for your room.

7

WITH THE MUSIC TURNED UP

It doesn't take much to figure out why everyone under nineteen wears headphones these days. When the beat is strong and the music is loud, there's nothing like it to get you in the mood to beat the drums of your heart.

Whatever your taste — jazz, metal, classical, rock, pop — music can get those lazy love muscles moving. Just shake your hips to the music and you will soon find you and your lover shaking to a totally new sound.

If you're a fan of a particular type of music, some corresponding touches can bring you and your lover to that high C note. That may mean the eerie light of

a black light bulb for rockers and the shimmering light of candles for lovers of the classics.

When it comes to really letting it all go and screaming out loud, there's nothing like a Miles Davis solo, some fast Santana, or Ravel's *Bolero* to bring out the beast in your soul. Wake that beast and you may find sex is something you feel from your head to your toes.

If that's not enough to get your lover dancing to the same tune, try kicking up the volume just a notch. No matter how tone deaf your lover may be, deep down in their soul is a tune that will get their heart singing. Keep playing that tune until your bed starts to rock and roll.

8

AT WORK

It's always wise to remember that all work and no play makes for a dull partner. If you can't get your mate to leave the office early, the solution may be to just do it at work.

Doing it at work doesn't mean you and your lover have to work at the same place, though that adds significantly to the possibilities. If you don't happen to work together, arrange to meet at one of your offices and head to the nearest hallway closet or empty conference room.

Like other ways of open and public enjoyment, making out at work carries some risks. Besides the danger of discovery, you may annoy the boss, or worse, make them jealous. But like most business decisions, it's the risk that makes the excitement and the reward.

The best surfaces for fun at the office include desktops, freight elevator floors, and bathroom stall walls. While you're being a busy body in an amorous project, don't forget to avoid leaving any body part prints that may cause later embarrassment.

Lovemaking at work can be brought up a level by a seductive lunch or dinner beforehand. Eat at the best restaurant near one of your offices, put it on your expense account, and head back for a roll in the memos. But be careful it's your tush and not your career that gets screwed.

9

WITH A TOY

Though your lifestyle may afford you various adult toys, taking many of them to bed could be uncomfortable. While your Ferrari may be a sexual stimulant parked on the side of the road, parked in the bedroom it could make for a few logistical problems.

Not to worry. There are plenty of little adult toys that work wonders in the bedroom. From simple French ticklers to whips and chains, there is an ever-growing supply of novelty and serious accessories for seriously fun sexual play. Combining use of a toy with the right viscous or sticky fluid may even bring tickles to places you never knew were tickle zones.

If you're beginners or a little cautious when it comes to lovemaking add-ons, try a vibrator. An old and reliable standard since the dawn of disposable batteries, the vibrator's buzz can be as exciting as honey to a bee. As always, exercise caution when using any electric or battery powered toy; you don't want to light up your block, just you and your partner, and maybe your bed.

Lovemaking toys don't have to be store bought, either. A cool sponge makes a neat way to soothe a lover, and an old-fashioned pillow fight can be exciting in the nude. If that doesn't get you, be creative. Try a little hide and seek until you've found every spot that turns your lover on.

10

TO BE PLEASED

There's not a lover who doesn't want to be pleased when it comes to making love, and letting your lover please you is like ordering room service and not moving from the bed. Tell your lover you're in the mood for a little bedroom service and just lie back and enjoy.

Doing it to be pleased allows your lover to be the ultimate giver. Whatever your taste — from scratching an itch to readjusting your back with a little massage — letting your lover give you the attention you need should give them as much pleasure as it does you.

Of course, you may find it hard, shall we say, for you to lie still under your lover's care. But go with the flow — you deserve it. Your lover certainly realizes that when they turn you on, they'll soon be feeling just as excited.

Be sure to tell your lover with the sweet sounds of your voice how much you're enjoying the extra bedroom courtesy. The expression of the pleasure you're feeling will inspire your lover to greater heights of pleasure for themselves.

Don't put a time limit on a trip to your lover's spa of love. Soak up all the excitement as long as it's given. You'll soon find you want to make it a regular excursion.

11

TOUCHING NEW PLACES

Every lover has their favorite spots on their lover's bodies that they return to again and again. But doing it by touching new places can stimulate sensations neither of you knew you could feel.

If you're a lover of thighs or chests, perhaps turn to the back of the neck or the arms. God gave man and woman lots of parts to use and to love, so don't let any go to waste.

The most obscure part of your lover's body can hold the key to lovemaking bliss. They may have a secret fetish for being stroked on the insides of their calves, the backs of their hands, or the base of their spine. Find that special spot and go to town.

There's no science to unearthing new places that can make you crazy with lust; it's an art. And like all good art, practice makes perfect. While it may take a few tries for you to nail down that new erogenous zone, the searching should be a lot of fun. Though you both may be a little shy about looking for new excitement stops on your bodies, a little gentle guidance can break the ice. Take your lover's hand and patiently guide them around the map of your body and have them do the same for you. See how many times each of you can find the path to your souls.

12

BEFORE GOING OUT

It's Saturday night and you and your lover are set to go out. When it's time do go, don't — head for the couch or the bedroom and share a quickie on the way out. Sex before going out adds a whole new perspective to an evening together, especially if you're heading to a place with lots of people. With a little lovemaking behind you, you and your lover can share gentle and knowing smiles while the party goes on.

What's more, doing it before going out improves the strength of your relationship. When you both have just acknowledged whom you want with a roll in the hay, even being surrounded by the most beautiful people makes them look dull. In a crowded restaurant or bar, your lovemaking bond will make you feel it's just the two of you there, no matter how many people wander by.

Making love before you go out can be part of a steady sexual diet or it can be an unannounced surprise. There's nothing like warming up for a big evening with a little appetizer of lovemaking.

If you're going somewhere fancy, dressing up beforehand may be part of the attraction. Grab your lover from the doorway, pull off those clothes, and turn on those bedroom eyes.

13

WITH SOMETHING COLD

If your lover's the Ice Queen or King, you may want to give them a dose of their own medicine to wake them from their sexual sleep. Doing it with something cold may be the shock to their system they need to get all heated up. Break out something from the refrigerator or freezer, bring it into the bedroom and set them free.

For purists, there's plain ice or ice water, or if you're health conscious, bottled water. Pour it on or rub it in until it tingles.

Equally stimulating to some is an ice cold shower or bath. While a hot shower or bath can have a sedating or relaxing effect, a cold one can give your flesh an electric feeling all over.

The standard bearer for doing it with something cold has to be ice cream. Whether it's with nuts on top, with whipped cream, or just straight out of the carton, a scoop of chocolate chip will give your lover the chilly thrill that chips them out of their icy love-making state.

Experts on the act of love have long known that the brain's pleasure center is close to its center of pain, and doing it with something cold seems to break lovers out of their Siberian freeze. Maybe that's why they say something too cold to bear can also be too good not to share.

14

WHEN YOU'RE ALL TIED UP

If keeping your lover's attention in bed is like getting toothpaste back in the tube, then doing it tied up may be the tie that binds the person you're tied to. From a silk scarf to a set of steel handcuffs, holding your lover tight may provide them a tantalizing tight fit.

For that matter, you may like getting tied up while your lover has their way with you. Being tied up can be experience the two of you will never for-

get. With one partner's hands or feet bound, the urge to be free and to enjoy sex at the same time yields powerful cross-currents that many couples find a tremendous turn-on.

The reasons, of course, lie deep in the subconscious mind. Not even Sigmund Freud could resist a serious feather stroking with his hands tied gently to the bedposts. And even the most jaded of lovemakers may find their juices boiling when forced into submission by kind but controlled caresses.

Being tied up is not for everyone — some may find it constrains their style — and it's important to set your lover free the instant they start to feel truly uncomfortable. Still, with gentleness, even the most restrained lover can be coaxed into tying the knot. After that, it may be getting them out of their perpetual smile that proves difficult.

15

IN THE MORNING

While most couples wake to the blare of the radio alarm, many choose a more healthy morning call. As the sun makes its way through the blinds and the noise in the street stirs, these couples spend time stirring in another way.

Indeed, what could be more healthy than getting your creative and other juices flowing before work or the day's chores? That way, come the afternoon when you're dread-

ing the rest of the day at work or taking care of the kids, you can just relish how nice the early morning was.

If you're not a morning person, doing it in the morning may change your mind about that time of the day.

You may quickly realize why everyone else in the office can somehow manage to smile before lunch.

Technique for the morning must be somewhat refined, as waking muscles take time to arouse. For those who like a little morning surprise, there's nothing like waking up to the inner rumblings of your body caused by a lover's touch.

You may want to make morning lovemaking like taking tea in the afternoon — a romantic ritual tying you to a time of the day when everything else is put aside. So much of our life is caught up in petty, meaningless things; starting the day off with a bang can make it all right.

16

BLINDFOLDED

"Close your eyes and I'll kiss you," the Beatles sang, and millions of young girls screamed. Let your lover blindfold you and you, too, will be screaming with delight. Blindfolding a lover is doubly exciting, for you and for your lover. The one blindfolded has the thrill of anticipation while the other becomes almost a voyeur to the captive partner's pleasure.

Almost anything soft will do for a blindfold, be it a dark scarf or an old piece of cloth. If you or your lover don't like the sensation of something tied on, then find an old style sleeping mask, which may be more comfortable.

In theory, the blindfolded partner will become more passive, once restrained by the lack of sight. But that may not hold true for you. The absence of sight may actually inspire you to use senses and sensations you normally ignore.

For those with total trust in their lover, the additional restraint of tying their hands together or to the headboard may add dimensions to your lovemaking all the sight in the world can't give.

Lovemaking blindfolded brings the mysterious element of the dark to the mysterious elements of sex. Of course, always be careful when in the dark to slip into ecstasy and not off the bed.

17

ON THE FLOOR

When "boring" becomes an adjective to describe your sex life, it's time to change your bedroom routine. Chances are lovemaking in the same old place — your bed — may have become as cut and dry as changing the sheets every Saturday morning.

Rerouting your normal lovemaking location to get down to the ground is as easy as doing it right on the floor. Whether it's the waxed parquet in the bedroom, the kitchen linoleum, or the bathroom tile, there's nothing like a quick and dirty on the flat and shiny.

If you think about it, it's not hard to see why lovemaking with your bottom to the earth is as nat-

ural as a bull kicking up dirt in a farmhouse stall. After all, take our friends in the animal kingdom. Have you ever seen two neighborhood cats or dogs run to their beds before getting down to business?

Perhaps you shouldn't either. When the urge grabs you, drop down and do it. So long as there's not traffic going by, you just may find that getting back to Mother Earth is what gets you going. In the backyard or in the hallway, gravity's pull may pull you deeper into orgasmic bliss. Add your favorite love lubricant and getting down to get down may make messy kitchen floor cleanup a lovemaker's joy.

18

WITH GUESTS NEXT DOOR

Almost like baring it all for strangers and doing it with a pal, doing it with guests next door is like sneaking a kiss in the stairway in school. Though the world outside may seem as if it knows what's going on, you and your lover know better. Because if they really knew what you were doing, they would be doing it, too.

When friends or relatives are over, either at a party or for the night, or when you happen to be in the same position at their place, it's time for a little positioning yourselves. While you don't have to wake the whole neighborhood to hear your lusty sighs, having some-one in the room next to your love-making lair will give you the erotic thrill of an invisible audience.

That's because as the old say-ing goes, there's a little thievery in every lovemaker's heart, and doing it when someone is listen-ing is like stealing the thunder from a quiet night's sleep. Remember, all's fair in love, especially when you're in the mood.

Needless to say, doing it with guests next door doesn't mean you have to re-strict your activities to the bed-room. A quickie behind the couch where your guests are sleeping can turn a dull party into the talk of the town.

19

AFTER A LITTLE WINE

The sainted souls who distilled the earth's first bottle of wine must have known they had a hit as soon as they poured it into a glass. Wine brings out the devilish side of any saint, and chances are if those first noble distillers had the chance, they probably grabbed their mates and headed straight to the boudoir.

For many couples, wine is the elixir of love, the tonic of passion that puts suddenly poetic souls in the mood. Whether it's white, red, or rosé, a glass of wine can be the aphrodisiac that lulls you and your lover into a lullaby groove. Even light or non-drinkers can join in the fun with a few sips and a little imagination.

Some who like spirits before they're in the spirit may insist on a stronger brew, and that's fine. But wine has its own special place in an amorous life, perhaps for the same reason that it fills a glass or two at the altar. Truly passionate sex can be a religious experience, and a few sips of wine can move you closer to a place near the love gods.

Be careful, of course, not to go beyond your limit. You want to drink just until you have a light buzz, and then go and buzz each other. Whatever the flavor or the strength of the brew, by all means drink as much as you want of the fruits of love.

20

IN THE POOL

If it's not ninety-five degrees in the shade of your love life, maybe it's time to get back to the basic elements. That may mean serious stroking in the pool to put the fire back in your water hole.

Though you may not own a pool, you probably have access to one. Whether it's at your neighbor's, or at your gym, school, or club, moving your lovemaking action to a cool body of water will

make waves of excitement and stir up the ol' waters of love.

If you are lucky enough to have your own pool, combining your lovemaking with touches like glowing candles or a bottle of champagne offers the chance to cool off and heat up at the same passionate moment. After all, you've made it this far, why not go all the way?

For those feeling themselves about to spontaneously combust with the sexual tension of a hot August night, jumping in may be just what you need to set yourself free. Of course, for those with hot tubs, feel free to feel equally free.

If you're not fortunate enough to own your own pool, doing it in a community or apartment pool may provide the thrill of having another's eyes upon you. Toss your inhibitions aside and get going; the water's great for making little things look big.

21

ON THE ROAD

With modern life's seemingly endless pressures and deadlines, more and more of our time seems to be spent doing things outside the home — except, of course, for sex. And while sex has routinely been limited to the confines of the home, there are a variety of ways to take the pleasures of love on the road.

With new technologies like cellular phones and laptop computers, sex on the road

can have a high-tech feel. Though the two of you may be separated by only a few miles, the next best thing to being there may be undressing during a long distance call.

From the days of men going off to sea with wooden replicas of women to keep them company, lovers with mates on the loose have pined for their main squeeze. For you and your lover, that may mean interrupting a business trip with a quick escape to the nearest resort.

Or it could mean doing it on a train or plane, where a briskly taken love session can take the stress out of a briskly paced life.

Not only is doing it on the road fun for travelers, it's also fun for those who rarely leave their apartment or house. Rent a car, head into the country, and figure out the quickest route to the mating grounds.

22

SLOWLY & SWEETLY

Like cooking good pudding, cooking up a good sexual meal sometimes means taking it slowly and sweetly. A touch of this and a touch of that is a relaxing way to enjoy a batch of your lover's treats.

In fact, lovemaking for the human animal was probably meant to be like a meal. While women would argue that most men like to eat fast food in bed, there are very few men who would not trade a quick sexual fix for a slow and sweet turn of the immortal screw.

Take time to please your lover or to receive pleasure from your lover. Forget yesterday; forget tomorrow. As Rod Stewart says, "Tonight's the night."

Still, the annoying noise of day to day life does creep into lovemaking and it's tough sometimes to shut it out. Lock the door, turn on some soft music, and allow yourselves to let yourselves go. Doing it slowly and sweetly makes the act of love so much more delicious and sincere.

If you or your lover are not ones for a slowhand style, an occasional change of pace may prompt you to new discoveries. Let yourselves see what happens when you force yourselves to slow down. Turn down the lights, switch off the TV, and lie back for a heavenly ride.

23

WITH SEXY UNDERWEAR

In today's era of grunge and rap music, underwear has crossed the line from underwear to outerwear. Be it Madonna flash or sleeky silk pajamas, donning seductive underwear gets a lot of people hot under their underpants.

That's because there's nothing quite like the textural appeal of a hot body in hot underwear. For most lovers, seeing their partner in sexy underwear is an invitation into the seams of just what it seems.

Inviting should be the operative word when it comes to wearing underwear to bed. Surprise your lover in a pair of sexy briefs or panties and let destiny takes its course under the covers with your under attire.

Of course, you don't have to take off your sexy underwear to get off, so to speak. Just gently move aside whatever cloth, plastic, or leather gets in your way and seek your pleasure — wherever it may be.

Of course, if you're style conscious, you may want to start your soiree by wandering through the lingerie section of your neighborhood department store or boutique. Feel all the fabrics and textures, and then decide. Once you've chosen the enticing garments for your lover and for yourself, head straight home and play dress-up until you get down.

24

WAITING FOR EACH OTHER

The waiting has always been the hardest part for the hardest parts at sexual play. Put off a lover with eager eyes and an itch in their pants and you quickly see that when the iron's hot, most people like letting off little steam.

As an ancient practice begun in the East, waiting for your lover to reach the peak of pleasure has captivated bedroom participants since someone with a starter's gun said go. For some lovers, the thrill of doing it while waiting to climax is much the same as waiting for their lover to come home to start coming and going.

Waiting for your lover to catch your waves does wonders for turning the heat of anticipation into the sighs of a climax. Like two sexual trains pulling into the station at the same time, waiting for each other brings the promise of a powerful bang from that head-on crash.

If neither of you has felt that power, you may want to keep the neighbors from listening to the noise you're sure to make by making sure the windows are closed.

Of course, if waiting all night for your pleasure drives you up the wall, try alternating patient lovemaking with quick bursts of frenetic fun. Moving back and forth from fast to slow can leave you coming and going with fun.

25

AS PRACTICE

You don't have to be a maestro on the violin to know that practice — as in several hours a day — makes perfect in so many ways. In music, the arts, and sports, only the rare natural gets by without a few hundred tries before perfecting their home run swing.

When it comes to the ultimate sport, otherwise known as making love, a fifteen-minute tune-up does wonders for your game. If, of course, your partner's body is still a little sore from the yesterday's game and threatens to rain out today's, then a little rub down or massage should relax their cramped lust ligaments in no time.

For newlyweds and new lovers,

doing it as practice lets you both get to know each other better without the pressure of stepping up to the plate with the bases loaded. Still, even the naturals sometimes need to sharpen their sexual game. When it comes to wiping out a new opponent or implementing a new line-up, strategy, or position, practice gives the best sexual athletes a chance to really strut their stuff.

Don't be intimidated if you're a little rusty playing a new position or throwing in a curve. Like many professional players who tune up by rounding the bases before they hit the field, making love as practice for the World Series of Lust can be almost as much fun as the real game.

26

ALL NIGHT

If you listen to half of what most books on sex say, you have to be an acrobat to fully explore human sexuality. And while doing it in an alternate pose or searching for that new G-spot can be balls of fun, doing it at all is the first imperative.

Once you've broken that barrier, doing it all night becomes an excellent extension. Shut the door, have a nice, tall iced tea or coffee, and go to it as long as you and your lover have the strength to go on.

Don't worry, doing it all night doesn't require any special gadgetry or toys, though they may help. Whether you've made the commitment to your lover for life or just for the night, doing it until the cock comes up to crow may bring out the rooster in both of you.

There are a few tricks to marathon lovemaking, and one of them is forgetting the day ahead. There's nothing like the thought of the next day's chores to take away all the energy you should be dedicating to a gleeful smile.

For some, getting to an all night and all morning smile may require the guidance of a training manual, but like regular physical workouts, it should become easier after a while.

For most, though, all night sex can be compared to riding a bike — it all comes back to you once you get on.

27

AFTER WORK

When 9 to 5 has become a grind, there are few things like a good post-work meltdown. Whether you wait for your lover at the door in your best attire or you both race at each other the way you race for the door at the end of the work day, doing it instead of overtime brings rewards bigger than the biggest paycheck.

Doing it after work sets the work day apart from the rest of your existence. Just enjoying your lover's presence in some lovemaking mirth can set aside that oncoming *Excedrin Headache #79*. There's nothing like a hard night in bed to ease the stress of a hard day at work.

Even doctors agree that tension headaches often get the quickest relief when you put your mutual heads together and get down to business as soon as you walk in from work. You can add a new twist by waiting for your lover in a seductive fantasy outfit or just by doing it in your special work clothes or uniform.

For those with an immediate urge after the work bell rings, get right to it wherever you meet. For married couples, that may mean sticking some money in the kids' hands and sending them out to McDonald's for their eats. Put off your dinner and have a piece of your honey pie instead.

28

WITH A SEXY VIDEO ON

There's nothing that a little inspiration won't cure in a lackluster love life. If you and your lover find you need a little extra spice to turn a dying spark into a flame, one spicy dish to try is watching a sexy video.

From a heated PG to a triple X, popping up some heated action on the VCR may heat up the action in your main attraction. Whether it's *Love Story* or *Debbie Does Dallas*, you and your lover may find the added stimulation of sexy action on the boob tube gets the circuitry crackling in both of your tubes.

While watching all the contortions and combinations of some adult videos can make you jealous, that should be the least of your concerns. Remember, art imitates life and that should be your goal; go ahead, get a little artsy in bed.

Still, if the clinical nature of X-rated movies is not for you, try something more tame or romantic to stir the loins. Good movies produce great tension, and finding a way to relieve that tension can be so much fun. Turn on the TV and VCR and get into some heavy action of your own. Be warned that sexy videos can make you forget everything but getting the corn popping in the act of love. That can get kind of expensive if you forget to rewind the tape before you bring it back to the video store.

29

WHILE SHARING FOOD

Long ago, back when men and women thought food was actually good for you, sex and food were never too far apart. One look at any of those great old paintings of those great old orgies and you'll see just how important food was to the activities at hand.

After all, sex and food are just different branches on the same tree of passion, and a good measure of a lover is how they eat their meals. Do you lick the last drop of jam from your spoon or suck your fingers after you eat fired chicken?

You can learn to put passion in your lovemaking by doing what comes naturally. If the taste and sensation of cold raspberries drive you crazy, why not share that sensation with or on your partner? Try something cold like ice cream or other dessert items like hot fudge.

Even after making love, leftovers provide an excellent outlet for any leftover sexual tension or energy. Why not cool off from a hot lovemaking session with some cold melon, and then start all over again?

As with other ways of spicing up your sex life, imagination is always king, so why not serve your lover a regal meal in bed? If the cooking is good, you may find you and your lover soon cooking yourselves. Put aside the utensils and get to the meat of the feast.

30

WITH THE WINDOWS OPEN

s anyone with any citified sexual experience knows, there is an erotic pulse to the noise of city streets. Doing it with the windows open captures that energy and brings it into the bedroom.

For those in the suburbs and beyond, the erotic pulse of the street's noise does not diminish, but changes into slower, more subtle sounds. In fact, the sounds of the wild outside your window may just be  what brings wild sounds out of you.

Letting in the fresh air from outside is a relaxing and sensual touch that many couples enjoy while making love. It's great that we have air conditioning and heating systems to keep us cool and warm, but there's nothing like the hint of the wind to send shivers up and down your sheets.

Doing it with the windows open also adds an atmosphere where strangers, or even the neighbors, may be listening. In that way, it's much like doing it in public for all to see.

Who cares who hears your screams of delight outside in the street below? If they were so smart, they'd be enjoying the same type of carnal bliss. Besides, if they do hear your moans and groans, can you think of any better compliment than the chatter of neighbors attesting to your torrents of orgasmic ecstasy?

31

FOR A PERSONAL RECORD

ovemaking brings out the best in all of us, including the competitive urge to be on top, so to speak. Why not channel that energy into a lovemaking session aimed at setting your own personal record?

Take a day off from your golf or tennis game and play that day's doubles indoors. You can start, for instance, by seeing how many ways listed in this book you can do in one evening or day. Or

take one of the ways and see how many of your own variations you can achieve in one session.

Lovemaking for a personal record can even be the center of your daily exercise workout.

Combine your workout and your lovemaking and do it all under one roof. Set a personal record while you're doing it and you may never return to the gym.

If you've forgotten or never kept your personal record for making love, now is as good a time as any to start keeping score. For singles in the age of safe sex, it's a good idea to keep the number of lovers you have to a minimum, and sharing the maximum with one lover becomes a way to compensate for any lack of variety. Invite your lover over, set the stopwatch, and go, go, go for the gold.

32

IN A DIFFERENT POSITION

L ife's too short to do everything the same way, especially
when it comes to making
love. Doing it in a different position is a fun way to tie you and your
love in the quintessential love knot.

You don't have
to be a sexual acro-
bat to try a new po-
sition. But doing
it in a style other
than the one you're
used to can add the
energy of a nude
wrestling match to
what may have be-
come a dull routine.

Being in a
different position means you and
your partner will be seeing things
and feeling things in a different
way, and as the French say, *vive
la différence*! The new sensations
of a different position can make a

dull sex life exciting again.

In fact, you or your lover may
have been dreaming about trying it a
different way. Ask your lover about
any special requests they may have,
and then melt their heart by giving
them what they
want. If you, on the
other hand, want to
do it some way you
normally don't, ask
nicely, and you will
probably receive
your wish for a
positional fix.

To check on
the positions avail-
able your lover has
to offer, consult their personal want
ads. Then, turn to any good sexual
reference guide for the specifics
of the job. Don't be intimidated if
you think you can't manage what
you see; it should be fun just to try.

33

WITH SOMETHING HOT

Some like it hot, and many like doing it with something hot. From a warm waterbed to a heat-creating lotion, doing it with a few added degrees can add many degrees to your love life's temperature.

In many lands, heat is an aphrodisiac all by itself. Remember, they call it the "missionary position" not because the missionaries were doing it, but because the natives couldn't stop. Even in the streets of New York or L.A., when the summer heat is on you'll find the most air conditioned natives burning up the bed.

Some say the reason why heat is an arousing force is really scientific. Since heat causes extra blood to flow to the part of the body it touches, what happens next is usually pretty obvious.

If heat's a turn-on for you, try pumping up your lover's temperature with an electric blanket, especially in the winter when there's a little nip in the air. In any season, a hot oil rub can do wonders for body parts with sluggish circulation.

The more heated your passion, the more heated your lover's will be, and doing it with something hot can turn a stone cold lover charcoal hot. Try a steaming shower or bath before you make love. It may be just what you need if your love life's cooled down.

34

IN THE WATER

For many, the burning heat of summer is the time to renew their own internal fire. So much of that feeling relates to the freedom summer gives to being near or in the water.

Since the days ancient when mariners created mermaids to fulfill their fantasies, men and women all over the world have found a way to make waves in the waves. But you don't need fantasy to bring the sensual cool of the water into your love life.  Rent a canoe at a local dock and head down the river of love.

Part of the attraction of water is its elemental nature. Since our bodies are ninety percent water, enjoying lovemaking in a little H_2O seems to bring us back to our primal state. Take a day off and go to the beach or a nearby pond. Watch the water ripple, and soon you should feel your own ripples inside.

For new lovers or for old lovers, doing it by the water can bring you back to the simple pleasure of youth. Whether it was your first kiss at the beach or at the summer camp pond, love in the cool and blue should get you all hot and red.

If you can't get your bodies down to a body of water, stay at home, lie in the tub, and rub-dub-dub away your blues. In no time you'll be able to straighten wrinkled love parts and then start wrinkling them again.

AFTER A GOOD SCRATCH

Think about the last time you itched in a place you couldn't scratch. Remember how heavenly, how satisfied, how thrilled you felt when someone's fingers finally grazed that spot? Repeat that feeling prior to making love and you're halfway to satisfying another kind of itch.

A good scratch can begin anywhere any time. It's an incredibly relaxing prelude to the act of making love. After all, giving your lover a good scratch will set their attention free to attend to the call of your body's desires.

Start with the back and work your way down or up to any other areas. While you or your lover may like your scalp scratched or rubbed, you may also have legs that drive you crazy until some nails make their way up to cool them down. Try a backscratcher to get to those spots that just won't quit.

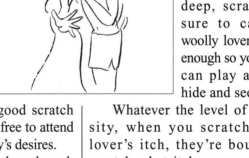

Try a gentle scratch to pacify a bear of lover by just lightly running your fingers up and down their skin. A deep, scratch is sure to calm a woolly lover's hide enough so you both can play a little hide and seek.

Whatever the level of intensity, when you scratch your lover's itch, they're bound to scratch what itches you. As the old saying goes, you scratch my back and I'll scratch yours.

BY CANDLELIGHT

From the dark mysteries of pagan ceremonies to the most erotic arrangements of foreign brothels, candles have played a part in lovemaking since humans struck a match to the wick of love. For you and your lover, doing it by candlelight may conjure up all those naughty spirits that make for seductive lovemaking.

Combined with other gentle ways of making love, doing it by candlelight will light the night for lovers with dark and dangerous thoughts. Whether you decorate the bathroom with different kinds of candles or bring candles or torchlight to your favorite nature trail, the flame of love is often lit by the flame of candlelight.

Of course, if either of you enjoy a touch of mysticism, recite your own special lovemaking incantation as you practice your ritual of love. Watch the flames dance and flicker as you set the ghost of sensuality free.

If, on the other hand, your lover is as conservative as a fire extinguisher, then try surprising them with candles surrounding the bed. While you may need to have a pail of water ready just in case, their passion may soar just in anticipation of the excitement to come. Whatever happens, remember not to let the flames jump from the bed to the drapes.

37

TO CELEBRATE

Whether you've just landed a new job, just set your personal best at the mile, or even just turned twenty-nine again, doing it to celebrate the occasion is an exciting way to top off a happy event. Every lover wants to feel special, and celebrating by making love will make marking any milestone a day you both remember for a long time.

After all, what better way to celebrate that sprint you made to home plate during the softball game on Saturday morning than with a sprint to the bedroom when you get home? What better way to pay homage to the day you made that million-dollar sale than with an equally powerful hand and body shake with your lover on the kitchen floor?

All-star lovers make all-star plays, and doing it to celebrate life's special occasions is a sure steal to a special sex life. Whether it's the first time you cooked Chinese food or the first Mercedes your lover bought, sex should be a part of the everyday celebration of being alive.

Doing it to celebrate will put your lover on a pedestal on their special hour or day. Of course, no one says that pedestal can't be the living room couch or the vanity down the hall. Take your lover by the hand and show them where the celebration starts.

38

ON SILK OR SATIN SHEETS

Much the way fine clothes make you feel good when you put them on and take them off, putting a set of silk or satin sheets on your bed can make you and your lover slide right into high gear.

Beds, like cars and other things that go bump in the night need sprucing up every once in a while for top performance. And there's nothing like silk or satin sheets to make the mere act of sliding into bed a thrill all by itself.

A touch of tradition from the playboys of the '50s and '60s, silk and satin sheets have lately come back into style. That's because not only will the cool, sensual touch of the silky fabric against your skin titillate every pore of your body, the royal feeling you get lying there is enough to make you want to stay, and stay, and stay.

Why not get a variety of silk or satin colors and styles to dress up before dressing down? Or, try shades or patterns that match your nightly attire to make your nightly action that much more exciting.

Doing it with silk or satin sheets will send your lover a strong signal that your bed is dressed for success. Remember, you go to all that effort to dress and undress your body, why not dress your bed for the part as well?

39

IN A DIFFERENT ROOM

Despite the best of intentions of the best of participants, a conventional sex life can come as close to dull as Siberia is to cold. To add a bit of the exotic erotic to your sexual ritual, let your mind wander and your body with it over to the next room.

Why relegate lovemaking only to the bedroom? While you can start in the bedroom, gently take your lover by the hand, kiss and caress your way down the hall, and get right to it in another room.

A great place, especially if you live with roommates or kids running around, is in the bathroom. Either with the water running in the shower or right there on the seat of the john, doing it against the cold, slick tile, plastic, and porcelain surfaces gives lovemaking in the bathroom a chintzy but highly erotic feel.

Another great place is in the kitchen, where the kitchen table makes a great odd piece of furniture for making love. You just may mash those dinner potatoes without a potato masher.

If worst comes to worst and you can't make it outside your bedroom for a little fun, then borrow a friend's or neighbor's favorite love hideout to play some lovemaking leap frog. Of course, be sure in all your activity that you don't break the Ming vase.

40

WITH SOMETHING SLIPPERY

Like the snake that tempted Eve in the Garden of Eden, you can tempt your lover to carnal knowledge with something slippery. From butter to scented oil to special love lotions, slippery substances make slippin' and slidin' in bed that much more fun.

Since the invention of virgin olive oil, lovemaking has always been associated with slippery substances — smoothing them on, rubbing them in, licking them off. You can slide your sex life that much closer to heaven with a smooth application of a slippery fluid or gel.

Margarine and plain old vegetable oil are fine like wine when it comes to easing into tight sexual corners, but for that matter, so is any household substance you can safely put in your mouth. In a pinch, butter makes a unique sexual flavoring, as does honey, jam, and jelly, though the latter three may be too sticky for some. Many sex shops also carry other slippery substances for making love, including lotions that have a flavor or that give off heat.

If you can bear the tire tracks on your bed, doing it with something slippery can add motion to the emotion of love. Take care and tip the bottle slowly. A little bit of something slippery can go a long, long, long way.

41

IN THE AFTERNOON

As anyone who has spent a length of time with one partner knows, sex frequently becomes solely an evening occupation. Even for singles in all their carnal glory, the pleasure of lovemaking often gets pushed aside to Friday and Saturday nights by the hectic pace of the work week.

If you're a lover in this position, a little afternoon ambush may be just what you need to break that dull habit. Who says you have to wait for love until after six? When the mood strikes, any time of day is the right time for making love.

Doing it between noon and five may just give you what all those weekday soap opera fans pine for — love in the afternoon. If you're used to doing it in the dark of night, then the afternoon light will give you the opportunity to look at your lover where the sun doesn't usually shine.

For late shift and night workers, doing it in the afternoon is the accepted course to intercourse. Many people with odd work times do it religiously in the afternoon — a great way to pass the time getting ready for the job.

For some, work is never an excuse to avoid having a ball making love in the afternoon. Why don't you and your lover make some heat off the job in the cool of the afternoon?

42

IN FRONT OF THE CAMERA

When the X rating of your love life seems to have dimmed to a PG, performing in front of the camera may wake the censors and sensations in your heart. Everyone wants to be a star in their fantasies and in their bedrooms, and doing it in front of the camera lets you be both.

With today's low-cost camcorders, doing it on videotape is an inexpensive way for you and your lover to feel like a million bucks. Whether you do it under the strict commands of an action director or just for the fun of creating your own bedroom viewing, doing it in front of the camera will urge you to the performance of your life.

While some lovers may want to pretend they're Richard Gere or Julia Roberts, remember these pictures are just for you, so you can be who you are. Of course, if doing it in front of the camera turns you on enough to give that extra effort in young performance, then you've accomplished what even the most ardent filmgoers wish for in their fantasies.

Don't forget to include your own fantasies in any sexy home movies. After you've had enough of watching everything your local video store has to offer, watching your own sexy movies may just get your lover up for an Oscar-winning performance.

43

UNANNOUNCED

You can sometimes put all of your effort into creating a romantic atmosphere, only to find your lover's simply not in the mood. Some people just don't respond well to an organized approach to romance. They'd rather do it as the feeling grabs them, so to speak.

If you or your lover are like that, think about doing it unannounced. Just start in wherever you are and whatever time it is. If you can maintain your sexual patience and poise, you're sure to reset your lover's lovemaking agenda.

Unannounced sex reaches deep into the heart of our animal instincts. In nature, just the smell of another member of the species sets off the spark of love. In humans, it can be the same way.

Right in the middle of the most ordinary activity, simply undress or begin to undress your lover. Then let nature take its course. You'll be surprised that even the most hesitant of lovers responds to a casually erotic invitation to sex. Some lovers don't truly enjoy sex until they're doing it. Doing it unannounced capitalizes on a reluctant lover's secret and perhaps latent desires.

While you may need the help of a prop or two to get your lover going, don't give up. You've got nothing but your clothes and your boredom to lose.

44

LIKE AN OPERA SINGER

While silence is golden for children and pets, it definitely does not add sparkle to sex. Sex is an expression of one's deepest feelings. Let your lust go wild and turn up the volume by doing it like an opera singer.

Making sounds during lovemaking lets your lover know you feel electrified. Why do you think women all over the world swoon when Pavarotti belts out a romantic aria, complete with sighs and moans and the waves of that little white handkerchief?

Don't inhibit yourself by keeping quiet during lovemaking. You express yourself verbally during the rest of the day; why stop expressing yourself when it comes to sex?

Share your feelings, your pleasure, and your passion with your lover by making the noises and saying the things you truly feel while making love. Speak in foreign tongues or by screaming naughty words if that's what turns you on.

Expressing what you feel, whether with words or through your own passionate aria, will help your lover know exactly what you like. You'll both get to see sides of each other that you don't normally see or hear. When people make love, they should feel as though they're on the top of Mount Olympus. Wouldn't you sing with joy if you were there?

45

AS THERAPY

When the bills, the boss, and your tennis elbow don't seem to want to go away, doing it as therapy may save the day. While serious problems and concerns can't be ignored forever, a relaxing dose of intimacy with your partner can go a long way towards easing the distress of the biggest of worries.

Sex is a release, and sharing it with an understanding partner can lift the weight of the world off your shoulders. In fact, put your whole body into it and you'll feel good from your head to your toes.

You may want to start off slowly if you've got a lot on your mind. Try something different like a little tickle or a few love taps to get you or your partner going, or just do what comes naturally.

If you both recognize each other's need for consideration and for pleasure, doing it as therapy can be a way for a gentle and concerned lover to express their concern.

Even when everything's fine, sex can be a great psychological tune-up. There's always a few physical or mental kinks we all have every day that kinky lovemaking can get unkinked.

Every once in a while we all need to feel that surge of power that only sex can bring. Plug into your lover's need to bring out the power of love.

46

AT A POSH HOTEL

When it comes to spicing up a tiring love life, there are few remedies as effective as a weekend at the ritziest getaway you can find. Be it in Paris, Rome, some tropical island, or simply the best inn your town has to offer, those few small amenities like mints on the pillows may move your lover to get the sheets ready for the maid.

There have probably been many times when you've said, "Things would be so much better between us if only..." When you leave home, all those "if only's" seem to come true.

You don't have to go overseas to enjoy the excitement of being away, but if the idea of crossing moun-

tains to move mountains thrills you, then head to your local travel agent and book the next flight.

Wherever you decide to make your retreat, have romance on your mind. Sightsee, dine on the finest, speak the native tongue and pretend you live this way every day. And while you're taking in the sights, don't forget how to speak those ageless words of passion, "Ooh," "Ahh," and "Yes."

In case you're on a budget or other responsibilities deter your plans, pretending may just have to do. Leave a "Do Not Disturb" sign on your bedroom door and imagine Robin Leach's voice welcoming you to paradise.

47

WITH THE LIGHTS ON

Most lovers like sex in the dark. But sex with the lights turned on can be a turn-on, especially if you can't remember whether that beauty mark on your lover's body is on their left or right hip.

Doing it with the lights on makes sense for couples who don't get to see each other often, too. Sex in the dark often tempts us into our own worlds, and doing it with the lights on allows lovers to get familiar again. You may forget what your lover really looks like in the dark. Turning on the lights lets you see all those glorious features that attracted you when you first met.

For those less eager to see  your bodies under what may seem the cold light, use a dim or soft bulb in your bedroom lamp. Dim, soft light will bring out a romantic quality to your lover's looks.

Other lovers may like their bedroom lit up like Broadway, and that can be very exciting, too. You may want to even go so far as to install track lighting in your bedroom, and why not? Lovemaking should be center stage for you both.

If you or your lover happens to be shy under the lights, that may be cause enough to turn them on. Grab your lover, give them a kiss, and tell them you want to see their glorious smile.

48

LIKE IT'S A DATE

Life is funny. Through all the things we do and see every day in our lives and relationships, sometimes we forget just how precious moments like our first date are.

The next time you're with your lover, why not pretend you're out on a date? It can be a one-night stand or the new beginning of a lifetime love. Let the magic that sparked your relationship spark new flames of desire. The anticipation of readying yourselves

to do it like it's a date is sure to get you pumped and excited at the prospect of getting excited and pumped.

Go all the way in recreating that first night you went all the way. If you still live in the same town, go to the same place and share the same things again, including the wine, the flowers, and the chocolates.

Why not even relive your date in the same clothes you wore that first time, whether they were tie-dyes or disco shoes? Remember, like fashion, when it comes to lovemaking what comes around, goes around again and again and again.

But you don't have to go to all that effort to do it as if it was that first date. For married and long-time couples especially, just the commitment to making a formal date with your lover can be enough to renew those feelings that made your heart race and your palms sweat during that first kiss.

49

WITH DIFFERENT NAMES

You don't have to be living under an alias to appreciate that sometimes it's fun to be called a name other than your given one. In lovemaking, using different names can provide an air of mystery and eroticism.

Many lovers have pet names for each other and there's no reason why you shouldn't use yours in your lovemaking rituals. Especially if your lover doesn't like their given name, using a different name when you make love may be the music of passion to your lover's ears.

Of course, you needn't use just pet names, though pet names can become pet names that you use when you pet. You can also use special names, such as those of famous actors or actresses.

Those who like to tease can find using special names during lovemaking an exciting way to stimulate your lover. If your usual fare is egging on your lover's passion through playful fun, then calling your lover by a different name may add significantly to the thrill.

In using different names during lovemaking, be careful you don't go too far and call your lover by the name of an ex-lover. If that happens by acci-dent, take the Fifth or plead that passion drove you temporarily insane.

50

OUTDOORS

What would a great sex life be without an occasional trek through the great outdoors? In the bushes, forest, mountains, or jungle, making love outdoors gives your body the fresh air you need to really breathe deep. No matter the season, doing it to the call of the wild will get you and your lover shrieking a wild call. On the slopes on a ski trip or in the backyard on a lark, making love outdoors in the winter is what's keeps Eskimos smiling even in those dark and long igloo nights.

In the spring, as in the summer and fall, the outdoors may be more conducive to your lovemaking style. Plan a hike in the mountains or make out in the neighborhood park; it's all the same great feeling of getting back to basics and doing it in the raw.

For adventurous lovers, try it on the ocean or the nearest body of water. Rent a sailboat for the night and lie out on the deck to enjoy the stars above you and the waves beneath your derriere. Others may want to try it on a deserted beach.

For those trapped in a cement jungle, the next best thing to doing it in the sands of the Sahara may be a wild jaunt on your balcony or apartment building roof. But wherever you decide to answer the mating song of your lover, take the next available plain, train, or elevator; Mother Nature calls.

51

UNTIL YOU DROP

Let's face it, there are few ways better to spend a day, week, or month than making love until you drop. Though you may not have the inclination to even do it until the sun comes up, why let honeymooners be the only ones who shut the door and stay in bed until they can't?

Make one weekend a month your honeymoon and just do it until you drop. You don't have to be just married to do it, just committed to each other and committed to sharing some serious fun.

If you can think of anything but sleep or food after a few hours or days of lovemaking, you need a serious attitude shift.

Shift into high gear with your lover and just keep doing it until you change your priorities.

For men, doing it until you drop also means changing your lovemaking routine. You can't expect to be a billowing Mount Vesuvius hour after hour, so you may have to move to less demanding techniques like massage.

For women, an advanced course of lovemaking may require the additional love moisture of a slippery fluid. Remember, though, whatever the technique, be sure that when you close the bedroom door for good that you've got enough energy to sustain you through your marathon of love.

DO IT WITH YOUR SHOES ON
& 101 OTHER FUN WAYS TO SPICE UP YOUR SEX LIFE

52

IN YOUR SLEEP

Early to bed, early to rise may not always make some of your body parts so eager to rise. And while your lover might never dare dream of sharing their sexual dreams, they may find they like love-making in the midst of their dreams.

Doing it while your lover is asleep is perhaps the ultimate in sexual voyeurism, but who else and where else to be a voyeur than with your partner in bed? Make sure the alarm clock is off, then start gently and slowly with a little foreplay. For your lover, that may be all you want to do until they learn how to dream in full sexual color and dimension.

Using the slightest touch, you can use your mouth to rouse and arouse your lover. If you want to go all the way, that's fine. Just realize you may have to make time to continue the action if you and your lover find the call to love stronger than the call to work.

Of course, there's no reason sex during sleep has to be in the morning, either. If you're a light sleeper or sometimes can't get to sleep, what better excuse to have your lover join you than to awaken them with a little lovemaking?

Catch your lover in the middle of a sexual dream and they may not even wake up when you're finished. Just roll over and smile in contentment; you've done your job well.

53

WITHOUT USING HANDS

For many, the hands are like eyes when it comes to making love — without them, they'd be blind. But lovemaking without using your hands can be an innovative way to learn more about the rest of your body and its sense of touch.

Doing it without your hands forces you and your lover into movements and positions that will make you feel like a slithering snake crawling in the grass. And slithering off into a snake hole can make a snake charmer's night.

Doing it without your hands puts emphasis on other senses, body parts, and muscles, much the way closing your eyes or blindfolding them forces you to think of new ways to excite each other.

To try lovemaking without hands, you and your lover should start out in a comfortable position.

Don't make any rules about how much you can't use your hands since you may need them for balance, but try to get into the spirit of the moment as much as you can.

Use your legs, your head, and the rest of your body for caresses as you take the road to sexual discovery. As you and your lover break your lovemaking routine, you may both find erogenous zones you never knew you had.

54

AFTER EXERCISING

Anyone who exercises regularly knows the special feeling your body gets after a rigorous workout. Doing it while still on that physical high sends many lovers to sexual heights beyond the thrill of winning marathon.

Exercise releases a lot of natural body chemicals that can make for a powerful pre-lovemaking brew. You may soon find your sexual juices jumping to a chemical reaction more explosive than a neutron bomb.

Add a round of lovemaking to your regular workout cycles. Meet at the gym, go through your workouts, and then get it going on the way home. By the time you make it in the door, you'll find you're both ready to work out again.

To multiply the effects of a good exercise workout on your sexual workout, a vigorous rubdown after exercise will get your love muscles even more pumped. Needless to say, if you're so relaxed afterwards that your normal sexual routine is too much, just go with the flow and use some gentle caressing.

For any lover tied up in knots by the day's stress, a dose of exercise followed by a dose of love will make every muscle in their body sing. Of course, the tune you sing will depend on how hard you worked out before, and then, in bed. Remember, no pain, no gain; no work, no fun.

55

INSTEAD OF LUNCH

When a quick sandwich or a hamburger isn't satisfying anymore for lunch, you may be hungering for a meal of a different kind. If you can make it back to your desk in time, shoot home and do it with your lover instead of lunch.

The workday has its ups and downs, and the perfect complement to those moods are the ins and outs of love. What with deadlines and commitments, some  power lovemaking instead of a power lunch can keep you performing at your peak in so many ways.

Of course, doing it instead of lunch doesn't have to be only a weekday thing. If the kids or room- mates are out playing in the yard or down at the local bar, sneak off to the bedroom and sandwich your- selves between the sheets. If you don't want to completely skip a meal, take a little snack with you while you enjoy your lusty fun.

For com- muters, making love instead of lunch may be more difficult, so you may have to think about rea- sonable alterna- tives, like doing it by phone or by computer. Make sure the rest of the office isn't hearing or watching you get excited, and keep an extra button-down or blouse handy in case your lunch time mischief takes out the starch in your shirt.

56

FOR PRESIDENT'S DAY

If it seems like it's been four score and seven years since the last time you made love, the time is approaching for you to do it again. Since the time to make love is almost any time, when there's a good reason like George Washington's and Abraham Lincoln's birthday it's so much the better.

Doing it for President's Day shows your patriotism in the true spirit of the red, white, and blue. In fact, lovemaking on any national holiday gives you free reign to set off your own fireworks. Be it the Fourth of July, Arbor Day, Bastille Day, or even National Baker's Day, when the your heart's not quite in the lovemaking spirit, give yourself a flag raising excuse to raise your sexual flag.

What's more, holidays like President's Day give a lot of us the day off from work, leaving plenty of time for play all day and especially, the night before. Plan something special, unplug the phone, and make your day off yours and your lover's sensually private holiday.

If you happen to be warring with your lover, make doing it for President's Day a reason to call a truce. There's nothing like a good rattle of the ol' sabers in bed to settle a lover's spat. Grab your partner, salute the flag, and start a parade towards some holiday fun.

57

IN A FOREIGN LANGUAGE

In old movies, Charles Boyer and Marlena Deitrich charmed us all with their foreign accents, hinting of exotic places and exciting intrigue. That's because the fantasy of the foreign seducer or seductress dwells somewhere in the brain near the centers of sex and speech.

The quickest languages for picking up quick and dirty phrases are the romance languages, like French, Spanish, and Italian. Since almost anything said in those tongues just oozes sex, you're sure to leave a lusty sigh hanging on the tip of your lover's tongue.

Even if you usually have trouble with foreign tongues other than your own, it's easy to learn a few key romantic phrases. You may want to go to your local bookstore or library and get a foreign language dictionary. If that still sounds too difficult, try just speaking with an accent or saying what you want with body language. You'll soon have your lover as hot as a side order of pasta in garlic and olive oil.

With a small list of key foreign words, any lover with half an ounce of romance will fall quickly under your spell. Of course, if you run out of words just make them up or borrow the names of foreign foods. In no time you and your lover will be wrapped up like two cherries in a crepe suzette.

58

USING JUST FOREPLAY

If every day you and your lover feel like doing it until you can't do it any more, that's great. But for those who don't always have the energy to match your desire, doing it just using foreplay is an excel lent compromise.

If you're not quite in the mood to finish what you started, just using foreplay allows you to enjoy as much sex as you want. It's kind of like eating at a salad bar or having an appetizer and skipping the main course.

Doing it just using foreplay can also be a way to regulate your sexual diet. That's because while gluttony in bed normally isn't as dangerous as overdoing it at the table, sometimes the sexual urge can get

out of control. Doing it just using foreplay can hold off the ever randy to their next regular sexual feeding and can even satisfy those with the incessant urge not only for the appetizer, but for dinner and dessert.

Foreplay can extend for hours, all night, or into sexual techniques practiced by lovers who would rather take the love train all night than get off at a particular station. Where one lover is very much in the mood for sex and one is not, just using foreplay provides a middle ground where both can meet.

Of course, good foreplay like eating good hors d'oeuvres, just stimulates the palate. Keep your bib on and enjoy the rest of the meal.

59

PLAYING SPECIAL ROLES

Whether you have a secret yearning to be a French parlor maid or a Chippendale stripper, doing it playing special roles can make for loads of sensuous fun. All lovers have secret fantasies that call for real life enactment, and doing it under the guise of special roles is one way to live out those fantasies.

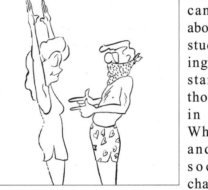

After all, the world's a stage, as Shakespeare said. Why not be each other's Romeo and Juliet when you step onto your own stage of love?

Try dressing up in the special clothes of your fantasy role or just playing the part in the buff. Whether it's imitating Bogart or Bacall or acting like Bozo the Clown, who says putting a little play in your foreplay is anything but fun?

Of course, while some lovers like their role playing a bit kinky, there's a variety of more conservative roles you can play. How about teacher and student, or casting director and starlet to evoke those lusty stars in your eyes? Why not master and servant or socialite and chauffeur?

Pick roles that excite both of you, and then close the curtains so the play can begin. Remember, whatever the special roles you each play to leave time for that special roll in the hay.

60

INSTEAD OF TV

Whether your taste is MTV or *Leave It To Beaver*, you probably spend more than a few hours a week in front of the television set. But unless your addiction to TV has been certified by a professional, flick off the remote, strip down to your skivvies, and do it with your lover instead.

If you think about it, when you add up all the hours of *Flipper* and *Beverly Hillbillies* reruns that you've seen, wouldn't you rather have spent that time making love? If you recognize Pee Wee Herman's features quicker than you recognize your lover's, it's time you cut the cable to the cable TV.

While TV can be a prelude to a

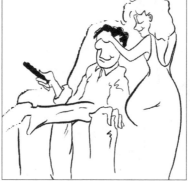

lovemaking session, when the time comes for the real action, turn your lover on instead. You've gotta' be a real couch potato to turn aside your lover to watch another juice machine or aerobic tape infomercial.

A compromise for TV addicts is to watch a sexy video for a while and then get into some lusty action of your own. You may even want to watch your own home videos to capture the intensity of a past traipse behind the drapes.

Make your bedroom activities a public service advertisement for a happier, healthier, and more satisfying sex life. Turn off the lights, shut the door, and create your own sexy prime time series.

61

AU NATURAL

While the entire non-human animal kingdom knows how good it feels to expose naked skin to fresh air, it's funny how we homo sapiens get so embarrassed by the naked body. Even those of us with the most beautiful of bodies seem wont to cover them up before getting it on.

But that's actually a good reason to get down to basics and do it with your lover au natural. Buck naked, butt naked, or just in the raw, doing it au natural brings out the animal in us all.

Sex without clothes offers the opportunity to rediscover forgotten anatomical parts. You'll be amazed at the riches a naughty little mind can find. What's more, doing it au natural requires no extra props or fancy accessories. If your work has you in a monkey suit all day, then make like a monkey at night and go bananas. Even if you both need to lose a few pounds, think, "So much lover, so little time." Get busy exploring every nook, morsel, and cranny.

For the squeamishly nude, there's more to life than a pretty face. Every lover has their good parts and bad, and doing it au natural puts them out there unashamed. Be proud of your body and your partner's. When it comes to sex, it's fun to appreciate a lover without a cloth cover.

62

AFTER A HIATUS

Like the cure for a case of tendonitis or chocolate overdose, doing it after a hiatus gives the body a chance to recuperate and to relish the memory. Lovemaking, like eating and exercising, often requires a little romantic pause.

In fact, a lovemaking hiatus will give you and your lover the chance to avoid intimacy when one or the other of you is not in the mood. There's nothing worse than making love with a lover whose mind is in another room, unless it's because your lover wants to be making love in that room instead.

Since absence makes the heart grow fonder, doing it after a little time off gives lovers time to remember that lovemaking is the most exciting part of being in love. For many couples, doing it after a hiatus gives them the energy to come at each other, so to speak, with new vigor. Even couples who make love frequently and passionately can get into a lovemaking rut. A lovemaking hiatus gives you both time to dream up new ways to drive each other wild.

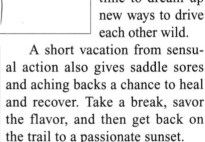

A short vacation from sensual action also gives saddle sores and aching backs a chance to heal and recover. Take a break, savor the flavor, and then get back on the trail to a passionate sunset.

63

AFTER READING A SEXY BOOK

From D.H. Lawrence to Anaïs Nin, stimulating literature makes an excellent prelude to lovemaking. The quiet anticipation of reading something sexy before lovemaking can be a turn-on whether your taste leans to the classics or to plain old trash.

For the intellectual but sensual sort, reading something sexy is a way to catch up on that French literature you never got to read in college. The charged atmosphere of a steamy passage can be your passage to a heightened awareness of your own fantasies.

Try acting out the most romantic scenes and don't worry if you don't exactly fit the roles.

You may not be your lover's fantasy lover incarnate, but remember, a fantasy lover can't touch your lover the way you can.

For those who don't read very often, find something easy to read. Just figuring out what that is at your local bookstore or library can be a turn-on on the way to writing your own passionate story. If books aren't your preferred reading material, any of the many popular sexy men's and women's magazines will do. Read the letters to the editor and talk about your favorites. By that time, chances are you'll both want to start something you can write to the editor about, too.

64

UNDER STRICT ORDERS

In lovemaking, as in life in general, sometimes someone's got to take control. Making love under a lover's strict orders provides the opportunity to assert that control.

As an outlet for the pent-up desires of a lover who wants to dominate or submit, doing it under strict orders will let normally submerged sides of your lovemaking personalities come to the surface. If that surface is yours or your lover's body, then you're on a good course.

Depending on how willing each of you are to obey your lover's commands, you can start slowly or go at army drill speed. Giving instructions to turn over or to address a specific part of the body are ways you or your lover can get the ball rolling.

For that matter, a little game of "doctor" can also be a good way to start. Write a prescription for vigorous sex and see that the prescription is filled immediately. Remember, unless you're both really into it, the dominant partner should still be as gentle as they would during any lovemaking session.

Needless to say, when making love under strict orders, the word "stop" uttered by either partner is an inviolable command. Still, when the action gets going hot and heavy you may be both so caught up in the spirit that neither of you ever wants to surrender the mood.

65

IN UNIFORM

Like a lover dressed in their formals, a lover in uniform seems to have passion at their command. From military officers to firefighters to bus drivers, a lover in full regalia can make you wish they were on parade just for you.

If you or your lover don't wear a uniform, then doing it in uniform may require a little costume work. Whether you dress like General Patton or Florence Nightingale, the thrill of your lover in a uniform may get you right where you put your underwear on.

If you do happen to wear a uniform, then by all means take it to bed. Starting there, you may want to combine your lovemaking with

exciting tales from work, like the time you or your lover fixed that kitchen pipe for that customer who was wearing nothing but a smile.

Of course, if the job hasn't taken you to places you consider exciting, then spin some erotic stories as you go. Carry the game one step further by acting your tales out or by calling each other by the title your uniforms demand.

Lovemaking with a lover in uniform can also be license for that lover to do what they do best. You may want to be the hapless speeder who gets pulled over and winds up submitting to a strip search. Don't ignore your rights as an offender — you can still get off on the road to love.

66

WHEN THE REVOLUTION COMES

What with war and strife an apparent never-ending fact of life, liberating your lover with some personal attention is an excellent way to calm their political concerns. When the next revolution comes, grab your lover, lock the door, and do it all night until you free your souls.

While your lover may be concerned day and night with the plight of Afghani rebels or Peruvian guerrillas, the politically correct thing to do during political crises is to add the human touch to both world and personal affairs.

For those who couldn't care less about what goes on in the world out-

side their bedroom, doing it when the revolution comes may give you a good excuse to celebrate with a little lovemaking bliss. Of course, if nothing but the call to arms is on every channel on TV, then it may just be time for you to put a couple of sand bags by the front door and begin making love until a new dawn comes.

If, in fact, the revolution does come, that will have given you the chance to enjoy the last few moments together getting a little peace, so to speak. On the other hand, if after all your lovemaking tussles the revolution fails, you may just want to try making a few revolutions of your own.

67

ON THE PHONE

lexander Graham Bell probably wasn't thinking of lovers when he invented the telephone, but doing it on the phone is one way to connect when you can't be together. Whether you're away on business or just at the office, telephone sex is a quick way to elicit your lover's touch tones.

That's because phone sex is both intimate and distant at the same time. You may be hundreds of miles from your lover or right in the next office, but speaking seductive words of love into the receiver is the next best thing to being there.

Some lovers make phone sex part of their regular lovemaking ritual, and you can do that, too.

Like *E.T.*, phone home on the way back from work or the supermarket. Tell your lover to be waiting, willing, and ready, and warm them up with your best offer of love.

Of course, you and your lover may be confined by the lack of a moving picture when it comes to doing it on the phone. In that case, you may want to invest in a videophone or at least in a good color picture of your lover in the nude.

Doing it on the telephone can be foreplay for you and your lover if you're both in a rush. Begin by telling each other what you're going to do when you finally get home. By the time you get home, your bells of lust will be ringing off the hook.

68

TO RELAX

Staying calm these days can make you crazy, and doing it to relax can be the cure. When everything seems to be getting in your way, a relaxing hour of lovemaking can soothe your screaming nerves and put you in the mood to enjoy the rest of life.

The key to doing it to relax is to do it in a style that will get you calm as the surface of a pond. That may mean doing it until you can't anymore or just doing it as a therapeutic way to release some pent-up tension.

In that sense, the speed and force of your lovemaking efforts should vary with how much you need to rock the boat, though putting it into full throttle may just be what you and your lover need to calm your restless seas.

Since sex to relax can become as therapeutic as a nice bath, you and your lover may find that making regular appointments to do it can augment whatever other special relaxing routines you already have. It's always nice to know that part of your regular relaxation mode includes the ultimate way to relax.

If that also means a little rubdown or some calming soft light, why not combine the two and really put yourself at ease? Relaxing together with a little intimacy will bring you as close as two peas in a pod. Put your bodies together and plant the seed of love.

69

LIKE AN ITALIAN

When it comes to passionate lovemaking, there are few people on earth as expressive as the Italians. Making love in Italy means bringing all of your body and soul into the act of love, and doing it like an Italian should bring you and your lover close to feeling as if you're floating away on a gondola in the canals of Venice.

Italians are so good at lovemaking because they bring all of human existence into their passion. Whether it's food or alcohol or anything else that turns your passion on, you may find doing it while munching on a Caesar Salad or after sharing a glass of chianti turns you into a romantic pair a la Sophia

Loren and Marcello Mastroianni.

Even if you're not an Italian or have never even met one, doing it like an Italian can add spice to your sex life. If you have to pretend, that's fine, because you may find that soon you're not pretending at all. While lovemaking at its most passionate knows no ethnic, racial, or religious bounds, making love with a touch more amore lets you lose yourself in the act of love.

Lovemaking Italian style can be as spicy as a good sausage and pepper dish. Like adding a little basil or oregano to your favorite food, it's the spice that so often gives lovemaking its flavor and zest.

70

WITH LITTLE LOVE TAPS

They say there's a fine line between pleasure and pain, and lovemaking with little love taps can turn the casual sting of a lover's palm into an erotic sensation.

You don't have to be the Marquis de Sade to enjoy a little pat on the rear during your lovemaking sessions. Many lovers are excited when bare hand touches bare flesh, and you may find it stimulating as well.

Doing it with little love taps may work best when it comes as a change in your lovemaking routine. The novelty of a little controlled violence in the bedroom will send your lover off like a bucking bronco.

Some lovers may find that doing it with little love taps makes the perfect companion for doing it with a new toy like a little paddle or for doing it while tied up. It's sometimes that hint of the kinky that will push your lover over the edge.

But you and your lover don't have to go over what you see as the edge to enjoy doing it with little taps. Just a friendly pat on the tush may be where you want to stop.

Always know your lover's bounds before you start with love taps. A bit too much may make your lover's skin all red and hard not in the place that you want.

71

WITH A FRIEND

While things like money are usually not the best things to share with friends, sharing sex with a friend can be a meaningful and fun way to spread some brotherly or sisterly love. From the earliest orgies of the Romans, adding a third, fourth, or fifth partner to the lovemaking ritual has been a novel, though somewhat eccentric way to turn the heat up.

The reasons for this probably stem from the geometry of the ancient Greeks. While one and one may equal two in simple math, one and two gets a little more confusing when there are angles involved. Sometimes, confu-sion leads to that silly spark of fun.

Fun is not the only reason to let a tag team partner into your bedroom. For instance, if your neighbor happens to be a dead ringer for Kim Basinger or Alec Baldwin, your partner may start sweating bullets of love just from the thought of having them near.

Of course, your third party does not have to actively partici-pate to partici-pate. You may be turned on by just having them watch your intimate session. But don't count on them sitting on the sidelines. Because when it comes to playing in bed, some-times the more the merrier.

72

WITH SOMETHING STICKY

Bees buzz around the hive because they know something the birds don't — honey tastes great. In fact, almost all sticky things make terrific tasting love potions and lotions.

Some of the best sticky materials fit for lovemaking include jams and jellies. While you may think strawberry jam is meant only for a side of toast, it can produce a wonderful taste sensation when applied to a side of your lover.

If you're watching your weight or even making love to lose a few pounds, you may want to use something dietetic for your sticky fun. How about a dab of low-cal honey mustard dressing or a few spoonfuls of frozen chocolate yogurt if you like cold delicacies?

The great beauty of doing it with something sticky is the way it entices you into interesting lovemaking modes. One that's really fun is to just do nothing but lick up what you've laid on or to pay attention to only one section of your lover until you go on to the next.

Of course, there is a downside to doing it with some gooey substance — if you don't manage to lick up what you've put on, you may wind up stuck to the sheets. Stuck or not to the next day's laundry, making love with something sticky is a sure way to get a routine sex life unstuck.

73

WITH A LITTLE MASSAGE

There's nothing quite so soothing or so sensual as an erotic massage. Doing it with a little massage makes making love the song that soothes the savage beast. Massage can be done in many ways. From little karate chops to gentle rubbing, a bit of massage will put your lover totally at sexual ease. Even gently running your fingers up and down your lover's body will get them into a picture perfect lovemaking frame of mind.

There's no reason why you can't enjoy the fun, too. Tell your lover you're fit to be plied, and then let them go at it with all the skill they can bring to the table of love. What's sauce for the goose is sauce for the gander, and a little massage as a regular preface to lovemaking will make you feel as good as warm butter is smooth.

For those who want to take a more scientific approach to the art of massage, there are many books on the subject available in your local library or bookstore. Applying just one of the techniques should be enough to get a reluctant lover up and ready to go.

Massage may make you so relaxed that all you want to do is ease off to sleep, and that's O.K. Your post-massage dreams may be so erotic that you'll wake up and ask your lover to start all over again.

74

BY COMPUTER

The computer age has invaded almost every aspect of our lives, but when it comes to lovemaking it need not be a hostile invasion. With the help of a modem and a phone line, you can do it with your lover by computer.

Sex by computer is also an ultra-safe way of making love with a third party. There are a variety of online services that allow intimate chat with friends or strangers via a phone line. Like doing it directly via Ma Bell, doing it by computer gives you the chance for lust at a distance with your fingertips on nothing more than a keyboard.

For lovers involved with or married to computer junkies, doing it by computer is an excellent way to keep your lover interested in romance. Computer junkies sometimes become so obsessed with their computers that nothing else seems to matter. Sending a hardcore message to their hard drive will get their integrated circuits focused on a little integrating of another kind.

In offices equipped with electronic mail, doing it by computer allows lovers at opposite ends of the office to let off a little steam or to create some. Why not download or upload fantasies or requests for attention? Pretty soon you'll have the whole office coming to you for more than computer advice.

75

INSTEAD OF EATING

The call to love is perhaps one of the strongest natural drives known to humankind, but so is the call to the dinner table. The next time your stomach wants what you know your waistline shouldn't have, grab your partner instead of those left over fried chicken wings.

Making love instead of eating has lots of advantages. While eating puts on calories, lovemaking takes them off, and doing it instead of eating doubles the effect. Do it every day instead of eating and pretty soon you'll look like centerfold material.

What's more, you can throw out all those special diet books if you head to the bed instead of the icebox. You'll trim those pounds as every plate of love you take from your lover satisfies that urge for a bag of chips or a piece of cake.

Still, like lovers can't go without love, people can't go without food. Even the most passionate of those substituting a sandwich of love for a pastrami on rye need nourishment eventually.

In that case, it may be your best course to combine the two urges into one and offset the calories going in with the ones going out. Remember, when it comes to food and love, it's better to eat at the table of love than not to fit in the dining room chair.

76

WITH LOVING WORDS

Not every lovemaking variation works for every couple. Few, however, work as well as doing it with loving words. From a simple, "That feels good," to a passionate, "Again! Again!", lovemaking combined with a caring word or two can win almost any heart.

Some lovers arouse easily to the spoken word. Others need to hear whole volumes of French poetry recited before they even listen. Still, most lovers are somewhere in between. Why not try moving your lover's libido with moving and tender words?

Loving words can be spoken in a foreign language or with a touch of the naughty, but they should al-

ways come from the heart. Search out your lover's aural G-spot and ply them with words of love from their inner ear to their outer parts.

When doing it using loving words, how you say what you say to your lover is almost as important as what you say to them. Some lovers shrink from too much affection while others are embarrassed. With the right tone, you may strike the chord that rings their chimes.

Lovemaking should never be too far from love itself, and using loving words keeps lovers close. Dig down deep in your passion; in no time you'll find you won't have to say another word.

77

WITH A TICKLE

For most couples, lovemaking requires a little funmaking now and again. Doing it with a little tickle can be just the thing that hits your lover's tickle spot. Not everyone's ticklish, but in the right mood almost anyone is. Especially at awkward moments or during lulls in your bedroom fun, giving your lover a quick tickle may put them back in the mood for more fun. Tickling brings you back to that

childhood laughter that makes all lovemaking so sweet and pure.

You or your lover may even find that tickling during your lovemaking drives you right to sexual hysteria. You may be able to drive your lover right over the edge of lust with a few gentle strokes over the edge of their most ticklish parts.

You can tickle a lover with any of your body parts, or for that matter, with any of a number of helpful tickling props. You may both find that tickling combined with the right follow-up, like using funny pet names or toys, gets you both so excited that you want to start all over and do it again.

For a lover whose tickle nerve seems to have frozen, a glass of spirits may thaw it. If that doesn't work, try making your lover your tickle prisoner, and see how long they can really hold out.

78

JUST FOR THE TASTE OF IT

When you were kids, your parents probably told you that one day you would really start to like members of the opposite sex. They also told you to just taste your vegetables because they were, for you. They were right on both accounts, but they left something out — tasting your lover is good for you, too.

Straight and conventional sex can be unmatched in excitement if done to your passionate best. It

can also get a little boring if not supplemented with other forms of lovemaking. You may want to try experimenting a little with oral sex and pleasing your lover by doing it just for the taste of it.

It may take time for you to get used to doing it using your mouth as the main part of your sexual grip on your lover, and they may not be accustomed to having it done to them. Most likely, though, one of you has tried it in the past, so let that lover become the mouth of the south, so to speak. You may soon find you both want to make it an everyday routine.

Oral sex is great because it doesn't require the energy that normal lovemaking requires. It's also a great addition to a sexual menu as an appetizer or in situations where you need to work quickly. Do it just for the taste of it. It's like drinking a cool diet soda — refreshing and almost calorie free.

79

IN THE TUB OR SHOWER

Clean or dirty before you get in, doing it in the tub or shower can be a sensually cleansing experience that keeps your body parts soft and shiny even as they get hard and warm.

In the tub, lovemaking has the relaxing, playful feel of an outing at the beach or country club without the embarrassing problem of sand and people in the wrong places. Of course, if your tub is small, you may be forced into a new way of doing things, such as a new position, or into just doing it as a preliminary before a trip to the bed.

For energetic lovemakers, doing it in the shower makes more

sense than in the bath. There's more room to move and the sound and pressure of the water beating down on naked bodies makes an erotic lovemaking backdrop.

In the tub or the shower, why not lather each other up or even give each other a shampoo? The sensual touch of your lover's hands will be unlike anything you experience at your hair stylist's or barber shop.

Yet, there's one caution for doing it for any length of time in the shower or tub. Besides the huge water bill you can run up, body parts soaking in the water tend to wrinkle and shrivel. Of course, that's easily cured with a quick drop of the soap.

80

JUST TO PLEASE

A sense of give and take is the key to any lasting sexual relationship. When your lover needs a little bit of tender loving care, making love just to please is always a welcome gift.

In the Orient, the gift of pleasure during lovemaking is considered the ultimate gift. Do something your lover especially loves, something you don't normally do, and watch them melt right in your hands.

For either sex, that may mean using a touch of the exotic, including lovemaking in a style you usually save for special occasions. If there's virtually nothing you don't normally do, then do more of it and do it better.

Gauge your performance by the smile on your lover's lips and the sounds emanating from their side of the bed. If you're doing it just to please, your pleasure should come from your lover's moans and sighs. Don't be afraid to let your lover become addicted to your amorous care. A lover treated royally in bed will usually return the favor in other ways.

For that matter, eventually you should be easily able to turn your lover's sexual pleasure into pleasure of your own, if not that night, then the next. In doing it just to please, tit for tat makes it just right.

81

LIKE A LIGHTNING STORM

While speed and power are normally thought of as assets in sports and in war, lovemaking at a forceful and frenzied pace can also be a powerful experience. Doing it like a lightning storm will give you and your lover a taste of that awesome and electric energy.

Like a thoroughbred heading for the finish or a tank tracking across dangerous terrain, putting all of your force into your lovemaking can power up a sputtering love life. Do it like a lightning storm until love starts to pour from your every pore.

Rainy days and nights are a great inspiration for lovemaking at such a raucous pace. Throw open the windows and just wait for the sparks to fly. If you hear the echoes of your sighs in the rolling thunder, you know you're on the right track.

Careful when lightning strikes in the bedroom, because all hell can break loose. You may find what started on the bed winds up being propelled down the hall.

Lightning storms can sometimes leave chaos in their wake; but don't look back. After the storm rains comes the calm of the warm mist rising off the ground. You'll find that lovemaking with the full force of nature can melt a frozen lover and turn them into a burning hunk of love.

82

STANDING UP

Making love is usually considered something you do lying down. As an interesting change, try doing it standing up. Against the wall or just holding each other tight, vertical lovemaking can make reluctant body parts stand at attention and join in.

While horizontal lovemaking has its advantages, doing it standing up almost forces the action. But in the vertical position, hands and arms are free to excite. Release yourselves from a lovemaking crossroads if you're always making love crosswise in your bed. Try it standing up and let gravity move your blood to those important parts.

Doing it standing up can also be more romantic and erotic, if not more practical for love at a horizontal standstill. So many movies portray hot bodies grabbing each other as soon as they walk in the door, so why not make your own sexy entrance home? Grab each other, plant a kiss, and let the clothes keep coming off until you're through with act four.

As vertical lovemaking may require a few warm-ups for lovers not familiar with the pose, caution is advised. Standing steady on your feet while the rest of your body moves requires a strong sense of balance and poise.

83

IN SOMEONE ELSE'S HOUSE

If you and your lover have explored every square inch of your house while making love, it may be time to do it in someone else's house. Like doing it under the watchful eyes of passers by or under the listening ear of guests in the next room, doing it in someone else's house provides the erotic sensation of others peering in on your fun.

You don't have to be a sneak or a cat burglar to do it in someone else's house. A visit to a friend's or relative's during a party will do. Sneak away or wait until no one's around, then get it going on the fancy sheets they save for guests. Part of the thrill comes from letting your hosts know you've done the dirty deed in their clean and tidy bed.

You can take the thrill of doing it in someone else's house to devious heights by doing it in every room of the house you've picked out. Put an ad in the paper offering yourselves as house sitters and you've got license to rock and roll. But be careful not to let the owners catch you on the way in the door from Disneyland.

Of course, the ultimate experience of doing it in someone else's house comes when you do it in someone else's bed. Jump in, get started, and make those mattress springs squeak.

84

BIT BY BIT

Attention to detail is a sign of lovers with an attitude normally reserved by most for work. Still, if you or your lover needs some attention to your details, try doing it bit by bit.

Exploring each other bit by bit is like sailing around the world first class. Each bit can be a port of discovery and the stopovers, little blissful retreats. Give your lover a taste of your passion in all the right places and they'll be sure to return the favor to you on a return voyage.

Making love bit by bit can be an adventure worthy of a couple of hours or a couple of days. Be sure to take mental notes all along your trip since each body part has a special way it likes to be treated.

The highlights of a head-to-toe trip through your lover's canals may be too much to remember for the next time, so you may need to make your own mental travel guide. Of course, don't forget the little bits that make each lover special. The eyelids, the nose, the toes — they all need attention, too.

Even bits hidden from the sunshine deserve special care. Use your hands and fingers to gently uncover those delicate sections of your lover's anatomy that never see the light of day.

85

WITH A NEW TWIST

Spicing up your sex life takes a little ingenuity and a little romance. Making love with a new twist will give you a bit of each. The key if you and your lover are in a rut could be the element of surprise. Pick a day and make that day special by doing something your lover doesn't normally expect.

That can mean doing it in your normal style but just changing the duration or the time of day. Whatever the variation, doing it

with a new twist will add excitement to your normal lovemaking ritual.

For some lovers, adding a new twist may mean throwing in something a little bit more unusual, such as doing it with a new species or doing it hanging from the dining room chandelier. For other lovers, a new twist may just mean doing it unannounced and without any prearrangement or plan.

It's generally a good idea to lock the front door, pull down all your shades and draw the curtains if doing something kinky is the twist that you and your lover crave. There's no need to alarm the neighbors or have them call in the men in blue.

Adding a new twist to your sex life can undo years of sexual boredom. Besides, what goes on behind closed doors between consenting behinds is for no one to judge. Break the ice, break the mold, and just have fun.

86

AS IF THE WORLD WAS ENDING

As everyday distractions take away from our passion and intensity, it's nearly impossible to make every lovemaking session the end-all for the act of love. Yet, you can instill that sense of urgency by pouring all your heart into making love as if the world was ending.

That's because a dull day doesn't mean that that day's sex has to be dull. When you do it as if the world was ending, every ounce of

your strength and passion will come out in the act of making love. At the end, you should be totally drained, as if it didn't matter if you died right there and then.

Gone With The Wind is one of the most romantic movies ever made, perhaps because of the Civil War chaos surrounding star-crossed lovers Scarlett and Rhett. You and your lover may find that doing it as if the world was ending will inject that same air of desperate romance into your sex life.

Even if it means just blocking out every interruption and annoyance that can spoil your lovemaking state of mind, doing it as if the world was ending will renew your spiritual and physical ties to each other. If your lovemaking has lost the spark of romance for a time, it may be time to pretend you hear the spark of gunfire in the distance.

WITH NAUGHTY WORDS

Every once in a while during lovemaking it's fun to let it all hang out, so to speak. One way to do that is to make love using naughty words. You don't have to use language you wouldn't normally use to speak to your lover in a naughty way. Just use whatever terms you need to describe what you feel or what you want.

Naughty words add a bit of titillation to your usual love language. Urge your lover on to more passionate heights with a throaty whisper in the heat of romance. Or turn them into a melting pat of butter with the right words said in just the right tantalizing way.

Using naughty nicknames can also make your lover's ears tingle. You can also describe certain body parts or features that turn you on by using naughty names and words.

If you like hearing naughty words when you make love, tell your lover to start the lingual action. In no time you may find you're both on the way to a storm of passionate, lusty sighs.

Make it slowly at first and see if your lover responds. More than likely, they'll join in the fun. Love and spicy language make good bedfellows. After all, why not let your lover know just how out-rageous you feel?

88

IN A DIFFERENT RHYTHM

In and out goes the rhythm of love, but if you don't watch it constantly, that rhythm can become monotonous. Doing it in a different rhythm can break through that routine and put your lovemaking into a different gear.

Like good dancing, good lovemaking has lots of different moves and grooves. With every different move you and your lover make, push yourselves to a powerful climax any lover would admire.

Lovers who are used to a gentle, quiet pace may find that doing it to a quicker drum may be enough to send them into overdrive. For those already at a speedy pace, slowing it down may give you both the chance to catch your heated breath.

Getting into a different lovemaking rhythm may be easierfor you and your lover with a little change of background music. Whether you need the sounds of African traditional music or a heavy Latin beat, doing it with a driving rhythm behind you can inspire you to lovemaking rhythms you never thought you could achieve.

Lovemaking in a multi-rhythm mode can get pretty intense. Before you put the CD player on random mode, you may want to make sure your bed is secured tightly to the floor.

89

BY THE BOOK

If you and your lover are ready and willing but need a little direction as to how and where to start, doing it by the book may be what's in order. Sometimes just a little bit of expert instruction is all that's needed to head to the top of the class.

Sexual instruction books are a good source of material for lovers caught in a quandary about how to catch each other the right way in bed. Whether it's directions on which physical shape or position your lovemaking should take, or just some advice on how to reach a better climax, many sex books can help you on the way to achieving your amorous goals.

For lovers a bit more experi-

enced, doing it by the book can give you both the opportunity to explore uncharted territory or to perfect your existing technique. Let one lover be the instructor and the other the student, and you'll quickly realize that school was never this much fun. If you're into role playing, try doing it as a command performance for a lover who wants a special show.

Of course, if you're not one to follow another's pointers, doing it by the book can be an interesting switch. Even if you start off doing it according to the rules, you may find the rebel in you gets so excited that you take a new direction to where no man or woman has gone before.

90

AS IF YOU'RE STRANGERS

When you first met, you were strangers. Revisit that special feeling by pretending your lover is someone you've never met. Strangers that you're attracted to always bring a sexual tension to a first meeting, and that's probably what happened when you and your lover met. You can recapture the erotic essence of that first meeting and rediscover your attractiveness.

Regaining your first erotic impulse to jump on each other may require a little romantic setup. You can stage an actual meeting somewhere romantic or just come at each other like strangers meeting for the first time in the bedroom.

For lovers who knew each other before they started thinking of each other as lovers, doing it as strangers may add a new wrinkle to a lovemaking routine providing no wrinkles in the sheets. Especially for lovers who have known or have been married to each other a long time, the thrill of seeing your lover as a flirtatious stranger may fulfill a need in you to actually seek one out.

For those who can see their lovers coming, so to speak, from a mile away, a little camouflage or costume may do the trick. After all, while love is blind, that doesn't mean your lover's eyes have to be closed to see you in a new light.

91

IN SPITE OF HOW YOU FEEL

One of the great benefits of having a strong and loving relationship is the opportunity it gives you to unload the frustrations of everything from bad days to the flu. And when those bad days come, doing it in spite of how you feel can brighten up your mood.

Understanding is the key to doing it in spite of how you feel. The tender touch of a lover may be enough to simply put you and your lover at peace in the midst of what seems the worst cold or the worst day.

Of course, it can be the opposite, too. Sex in spite of how you feel gives your body and mind the opportunity to focus negative energy on something extremely positive, sending you to heights you never thought you would reach any time soon.

It's important to remember that not everyone feels like making love when they're not in the mood, so you and your lover must realiz each other's limits. Still, being alert to your partner's love signals may be what alerts you to other life signals that can help change their mood.

If simply lying in bed has become the routine of late, why not make the time as useful as possible? You may be pleasantly surprised at how your bodies react to quickly change your mood and put a smile on your face.

DO IT WITH YOUR SHOES ON

& 101 OTHER FUN WAYS TO SPICE UP YOUR SEX LIFE

AFTER A ROMANTIC DINNER

Even for the most diet-conscious lover and those substituting steady meals of love for a bountiful feast, a romantic dinner can be an exciting appetizer for a main course of love. Lovemaking after a romantic dinner combines all of the best elements of sensuality — food, spirits, candlelight, and footsie under the table.

Start a lovemaking session over champagne and a filet mignon and your juices should be running like a lightly grilled steak. Go to a nice restaurant and tell the waiter or maitre d' to sit you at a table in the back. Make sure to taste each other's meals by sensuously putting a forkful of your dinner in your lover's mouth as you gently place your hand on their thigh.

Romance is an essential part of lovemaking, and the sated feeling that comes from a romantic dinner can be so relaxing that the only thoughts you both have are of stripping off your clothes and doing it right on the table. Wait, instead, for your bedroom if you can manage it, or go ahead if you think you can get away with it between the silverware.

Of course, your romantic dinner doesn't have to be at a restaurant. It can be right at home. Draw the curtains, light some candles, and choose your entreé from the menu of love.

93

AS A GAME

While we all know that playing games with a lover's head can lead you both into an emotional minefield, playing games with their body is a whole other experience. Making love as if it were a game brings out the sexual competitor in even the most reticent lover.

Trying lovemaking as a game may sound a little childish, but give it a go and you may find it works for you. Whether you use a point system for sexual performance or for other considerations in your relationship, a good game of "you show me yours and I'll show you mine" can be fun.

Sports fans will instantly be attracted to doing it as a game. Give extra points for extra attention to special parts or to special craves.

Of course, the oldest sexual game is strip poker, a perfect chance for new lovers to really get to know each other better. If poker's not your game, try strip chess or checkers if that gets your pokers hot. Why not make the rules so that the loser has to be the doer while the winner gets it done to?

Be mindful that while making love can be a great game, sometimes pride gets involved, so be sure to keep your lovemaking playful. It's always better to play until someone has a sore back instead of sore feelings.

94

INSTEAD OF GOING OUT

Some of the best times come when two lovers spend a night or day on the town. But if the weather's inclement or the movie lineup is dull, why not make love instead? Order in some pizza, share it seductively, and then head straight to the bedroom or couch and spend some quality time.

Doing it instead of going out can give you both a break from the ritual of dressing up and spending cash. How about enjoying each other while doing something noble at the same time? Donate what you would have spent on dinner to a worthy cause. That way, while you're helping others, you're helping yourselves to a pleasurable time.

Making love instead of going out on the weekends is also a way to get a jump on a marathon lovemaking session. Come Friday night, break out a nice bottle of wine, lock the bedroom door, and enjoy each other until you have to go to work on Monday. If you spend a few weekends that way, pretty soon the worst job will seem like a piece of cake.

If the prospect of doing it instead of going out doesn't thrill you, perhaps a shorter outing can suffice. Go out for a quick bite to eat, skip the ice cream, and head home to bed. After your detour, tell your lover the dessert is now due.

95

AS EXERCISE

Americans may be in the grips of a fitness craze, but let's face it, jumping jacks, sit-ups and pushups are hard work. Why not make exercising more enjoyable and spice up your sex life all at once by making love part of your exercise routine?

You can start integrating love-making into your daily or weekly exercise routine slowly by substituting a little love-making for a set of curls or pull-ups. If you and your lover regularly exercise at a gym, you may want to cut short your workout there and head home for a sexual workout. Pushups are certainly more fun on top of your lover than on top of a vinyl mat. For that matter, so is any exercise you can do with or on top of your lover instead of solo.

Lovemaking with the intensity of exercise should take off at least as many calories as exercise does, if not more. For maximum effectiveness, you'll probably want to go at a clip that immediately takes off a few pounds. You may have to work up to that pace, but it should be fun getting there.

Lovers into pumping up may find that lovemaking in various poses and positions pumps you into high calorie-burning ecstasy. If after that you're still not sweating bullets of fire, it may mean it's time for an all-night affair.

96

IN COSTUME

Life can be a carnival and so can making love. By combining a little touch of the bizarre with a bit of the risque, lovemaking can take on all the erotic madness of Mardí Gras. Do it in costume and you and your lover may uncover some of your most hidden fantasies.

If you or your lover has a secret wish to do it with Robin Hood or Maid Marion, doing it in costume gives you the ability to make that wish come true. Dress up like a cowboy and cowgirl and get out there and rope some pony.

If you or your lover are into the occult, making love in costume gives you the chance to per-

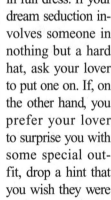

form your own version of some ancient lovemaking rituals. Light a couple of candles and recite your own lusty love incantations.

There's no reason if you're doing it in costume that you both have to be in full dress. If your dream seduction involves someone in nothing but a hard hat, ask your lover to put one on. If, on the other hand, you prefer your lover to surprise you with some special outfit, drop a hint that you wish they were delivering your morning mail instead of your regular letter carrier.

Whatever the outfit, remember that even when doing it in costume, it's still who you are that's important and not the clothes you wear.

ONLY WITH YOUR LIPS

Every great romance starts with a kiss, whether it's a peck on the cheek or a juicy tongue twirler. That first kiss remains special forever, perhaps for its promise and tension, perhaps for its directness and sensuality.

You can reproduce that feeling again in a big way by doing it only with your lips. Like an erotic bath of preliminary lovemaking, doing it only with your lips can serve as a sensuous appetizer for a full meal of love.

You can start with some easily removable clothes on and then remove them or even start naked. Begin kissing and patting and slurping with your lips until you're so close to using your hands that you can't resist. The sexual tension you'll build will make you realize how much more there is to come.

Try your erotic best to arouse your lover to a new sexual high. If things get so out of control that doing it only with your lips seems unduly cruel, then give yourselves the leeway to bring in other body parts as well. Doing it only with your lips is an excellent way to start your lovemaking action that builds on the tension of that great first kiss. You may even find you've neglected to view your lips as the sexual organs they are. Don't pout. It's easily rectified.

98

FOR THE WORLD RECORD

Once you've decided to commit to your lover, why not commit to being the best pair of lovers the world's ever seen? Doing it for the world record may put you in that league. Whether you set the record for the most times in one evening, week, month or year, imagine all the fun of preparing and training to get there.

You may consider the work of setting any of the world's sexual records too hard, so to speak, so you don't have to actually go for the gold. But approaching the limit of both of your abilities will certainly put new energy in your relationship, as well as in your cardiovascular system.

Some couples set new records every time they meet. Whether it's for the number of new gadgets used or for the longest time from foreplay to climax, these lovers don't need a coach to get them running for the tape.

If you and your lover feel you do need a little advice, there are plenty of good guides. You might want try going after the record for the lovemaking position that approximates the butterfly stroke in swimming, or chasing the record for the number of consecutive orgasms in a specified time. Whatever the record you try to set, remember that the international rules of love still apply.

99

AS A REWARD

Like giving a good dog a bone, good lovers also deserve a special treat. When you or your lover have been worthy of a love sweet, doing it as a reward can be the human equivalent of rewarding your favorite animal friend.

There are many ways to reward a lover's kindness or caring, and sex is one of the most wonderful ways. Especially for a lover who's gone out of their way to do something special, some very deserved lovemaking is always in order. For a novel touch, why not present yourself dressed in just a ribbon and surprise your lover with the best sex they've ever had.

On the other hand, some lovers respond best to Pavlovian-style lovemaking treats. If your lover has neglected their duties around the house, then every step toward improvement may earn a special love gift. Even lovers with the best behavior can be gently steered in a better direction with the gentle persuasion that starts with a kiss.

You may even find yourself the recipient of some hot and heavy rewards. Lovemaking has a way of growing on you when it's offered in a noble spirit, and doing it as a reward makes giving love as much fun as getting it is. Give your lover their just deserts and reward them with a love crème de menthe.

100

FOR THE GIPPER

You don't have to be Knute Rockne to appreciate that every once in a while you've got to pull up your socks and get back in the game. That also holds true for a sexual relationship that may seem like it's temporarily a losing cause.

Do it for the Gipper if that's the case, because you may be surprised at how quickly the score turns around. If your partner is at a sexual low, all you may need is a quick motivation lovemaking session to get right back in the thick of things. It may require the encouragement of some soothing, loving words, or the urging of some naughty, nasty trash to get you or your lover's backfield in motion.

That may mean ignoring the mood you're in and going full throttle, or just enjoying a love-making session as something to put your head back on right.

Since humans arose from the dust, few lovers have felt like making it together every day or night. But for those times when one feels like it and the other's less than sure, doing it for the Gipper may make sense.

After all, there are a lot worse things you could be doing with your lover than having sex, and skipping sex can become a hard habit to break. It's first and goal and you've got to get your lover across the goal line. Bend over, take the snap, and send them a pass.

101

FULFILLING A FANTASY

Love is but a fantasy fulfilled in two lovers' minds, a famous author once wrote. The same can be said of lust. Where the heart beats so do the sexual drums, and where your lover's sexual fantasies lie, you'll find the ultimate mirror of their soul.

Whether you or your lover want to do it at the top of a mountain or at the bottom of a river valley, finding and fulfilling that fantasy can bring you both to the peak of ecstasy.

Of course, all fantasies are not so serious. You may just have a foot fetish you want addressed or a desire for some whipped topping in all the right places.

Sexual fantasies are not always easy to fulfill. Sometimes they require the participation of others or their non-participation. That may mean a lot of advanced preparation to make the special scene your lover desires for making out. Just remember that the effort spent on fulfilling a lover's fantasy can unleash a torrent of passion that leaves you both totally spent.

Fantasies can also get expensive, such as those that involve a romantic dinner or a stay in a four-star hotel. Still, whenever you can make it to the core of your lover's sexual desires, you should find a place that's cozy, safe, and warm.

102

JUST BECAUSE

If you or your lover have no good reason to make love, then doing it just because is reason enough. Because of all the ways to spice up your sex life, doing it for no reason at all may be the best. When you and your lover can admit to each other that there's not much you need to start making love, then you've conquered emotional terrain few lovers ever reach.

Making love should need no reason besides how much each of you

cares for the other and how much you turn each other on. Think about how easy it was when you first met. You liked what you saw, you came, and you conquered. Today, this day, it should be the same.

All jokes aside, the only thing serious about making love is that it should always be fun, safe, and loving. Doing it just because reaffirms your commitment to your lover and to the caring and the relationship you share. After the gifts and the fights and the dates and the hard times, there's not much that comes close to the feeling of holding each other close.

Do it just because you love your lover, because you like them, because you enjoy their company and their body. We live in a crazy time and things can get scary if you really think about it. Turn out the lights, roll over, and kiss it all away.

DO IT WITH YOUR SHOES ON
& 101 OTHER FUN WAYS TO SPICE UP YOUR SEX LIFE

SEX QUIZ

In the fall of 1989, the renown Kinsey Institute commissioned The Roper Organization to poll the American public on their basic knowledge of sex. Fifty-five percent failed, unable to answer at least 10 of the 18 questions correctly. We've selected seven of those 18 questions. Why don't you test your sexual IQ?

1) Nowadays, what do you think is the age at which the *average* or *typical* American *first* has sexual intercourse?

a. <=11	c. 13	e. 15	g. 17	i. 19	k. >=11
b. 12	d. 14	f. 16	h. 18	j. 20	

2) A woman can get pregnant during her period. True or False?

3) Problems with erection are most often started by a physical problem. True or False?

4) Almost all erection problems can be successfully treated. True or False?

5) What percentage of American women would you estimate have masturbated either as children or after they were grown up?

a. <=10%	c. 20%	e. 40%	g. 60%	i. 80%
b. 10%	d. 30%	f. 50%	h. 70%	j. >=90%

6) What do you think is the length of the average man's *erect* penis?

a. 2 "	c. 4 "	e. 6 "	g. 8"	i. 10 "	k. 12"
b. 3 "	d. 5 "	f. 7 "	h. 9 "	j. 11 "	

7) Most women prefer a sexual partner with a larger-than-average penis. True or False?

Answers
1) 16-17   2) True   3) True   4) True   5) 60 - 80%   6) 5-7"   7) False

Adapted from the book, *The Kinsey Institute New Report On Sex,* by June M. Reinisch, Ph.D., with Ruth Beasley, M.L.S. Copyright © 1990 by the The Kinsey Institute for Research in Sex, Gender and Reproduction. Reprinted with premission from St. Martin's Press, Inc.

PLACES TO TURN

Each of the following four catalogs provide a valuable assortment of the most useful and high quality products to promote your sexual enjoyment and safety. Some of these catalogs require you to be 21 or older and to send a statement of age with your request.

CONDOMania: From the world's most famous and nation's first condom store, an interesting assortment of sexually oriented products aimed at promoting safer and more enjoyable sex. Included are a variety of condoms, lubricants, novelties, and safe-sex kits. Catalog is free. Call (800) 9CONDOM or write to CONDOMania, 7306 Melrose Avenue, Los Angeles, CA 90046, Attn: Mail Order Division.

Femme Distribution: A free catalog containing a line of erotic adult couples videos filmed from a woman's perspective. Call (800) 456-LOVE or write to Femme Distribution, P.O. Box 268, Prince Street Station, New York, NY 10012.

Sexual Healings: A variety of sexually explicit informational videos geared to enhancing and improving sexuality. Catalog is free. Call (800) 456-LOVE or write to Sexual Healings, P.O. Box 268, Prince Street Station, New York, NY 10012.

The Xandria Collection: One of the world's most popular catalogs of any kind featuring an outstanding, high quality variety of exotic oils, romantic games, playtoys, lingerie, books, and videos. Complete confidentiality and satisfaction guaranteed. Catalog is $4.00 (applied towards your first order). Write to The Xandria Collection, 165 Valley Drive, Dept. BK-1, Brisbane, CA 94005-1340.

INSPIRING VIDEOS

These five movies are among the best ever made for turning a night in front of the TV into a night you and your lover will never forget. All are available on home video and should be easily found for sale or rent in your local video store.

An Officer And A Gentleman, starring Richard Gere and Debra Winger, directed by Taylor Hackford, 1982. Winger chases Gere through a series of steamy scenes, including the famous chair ride. Rated R, 125 minutes.

Body Heat, starring William Hurt and Kathleen Turner, directed by Lawrence Kasdan, 1981. Turner, in her first film, entices Hurt into more than hanky panky. Great for late night VCR action. Rated R, 113 minutes.

From Here To Eternity, starring Burt Lancaster and Deborah Kerr, directed by Fred Zinneman, 1953. Adapted from the James Jones novel, an all-star cast brilliantly brings the tension of pre-Pearl Harbor Hawaii to the big screen. Includes the original "sex on the beach" scene. Winner of eight Academy Awards, including Best Picture. Not rated, in black and white, 118 minutes.

Last Tango In Paris, starring Marlon Brando and Maria Schneider, directed by Bernardo Bertolucci, 1973. Brando and Bertolucci make this somewhat explicit tale of an American expatriate in Paris a classic. Rated X (also available in an R version), 129 minutes.

Nine 1/2 Weeks, starring Mickey Rourke and Kim Basinger, directed by Adrian Lyne, 1986. A touch of the weird and the erotic featuring Rourke as a man obsessed with an incredibly sexy Basinger. Interesting, but not for everyone's taste. Rated R, 113 minutes.

MUSICAL FAVORITES

The following 15 recordings represent a small sampling of some of the great music that can get you in the lovemaking mood. Most are available on CD though some may only be available on cassette tape or old-fashioned vinyl.

Addicted To Love (Palmer) by Robert Palmer from the album *Riptide.*
All Blues (Davis) by Miles Davis from the album *Kind Of Blue.*
Batuka (Santana) by Santana from the album *Santana.*
Bolero (Ravel) by The New York Philharmonic from the album *Music Of Ravel.*
Burning Love (Linde) by Elvis Presley from the album *Top Ten Hits.*
Can't Get Enough Of Your Love, Babe (White) by Barry White from the album *Barry White's Greatest Hits.*
Do Ya Think I'm Sexy? (Stewart-Appice) by Rod Stewart from the album *Blondes Have More Fun.*
*Get Down Tonigh*t (Casey-Finch) by KC & The Sunshine Band from the album *The Best Of KC & The Sunshine Band.*
*Kiss You All Over (*Chapman-Chinn) by Exile from the album *Greatest Hits.*
Lady In Red (De Burgh) by Chris De Burgh from the album *Working Girl.*
Like A Virgin (Steinberg-Kelly) by Madonna from the album *Like A Virgin.*
Sex Machine (Brown-Byrd-Lenhoff) by James Brown from the album *Shades Of Brown.*
Sexual Healing (Gaye-Brown) by Marvin Gaye from the album *Midnight Love.*
Tonight's The Night (Gonna Be Alright) (Stewart) by Rod Stewart from the album *A Night On The Town.*
Wonderful Tonight (Clapton) by Eric Clapton from the album *Slowhand.*

FURTHER READING

These ten books will provide you with further information and ideas to help you towards a healthier, happier, and more fun sex life. Most should be available at your local library or bookstore or can be special ordered through your bookstore or directly through the publisher.

Delta Of Venus, by Anaïs Nin (Bantam, 1978, $4.50).

Fantasex: A Book Of Erotic Games For The Adult Couple, by Rolf Milonas (Putnam, 1983, $8.95).

Fear Of Flying, by Erica Jong (Signet, 1974, $5.99).

If It Feels Good: Using The Five Senses To Enhance Your Lovemaking, by Jon E. Lloyd (Warner Books, 1993, $10.99).

Joy Of Sex & More Joy Of Sex (boxed set), by Alex Comfort (Fireside, 1975, $33.90).

Lady Chatterly's Lover, by D.H. Lawrence, edited by Lawrence Durell (Bantam Classic Series, 1983, $3.50).

Sex From Aah To Zipper, by Roger Libby, Ph.D. (Playful Pleasure Press, 1993, $11.95).

Super Marital Sex: Loving For Life, by Paul Pearsall, Ph.D. (Ivy Books, 1987, $5.99).

The Kinsey Institute New Report On Sex, by June M. Reinisch, Ph.D., with Ruth Beasley, M.L.S. (St. Martin's Press, 1990, $14.95).

"Since I got HIV, all I want to do is tell women that love alone won't protect them. You have to protect yourself."

AIDS is a leading cause of death among women.

"I used to think that having a man who loved me would keep me safe…until I got HIV.

"But you know something? Most women still don't protect themselves. And I think it's for the same reason.

"Please listen to me. A man can tell you he loves you and that he'll never hurt you. But if he has HIV and doesn't know it, how will you?"

To find out how you can prevent HIV, call the CDC National AIDS Hotline at 1-800-342-AIDS.

AMERICA
RESPONDS
TO AIDS

Frankie Alston, HIV Positive

Getting Educated Has Never Been

So Much Fun

INTRODUCING THE WORLD'S FIRST HIP EDUCATIONAL SAFER SEX KIT

The Kit Features

1 BEYOND 7 CONDOM
1 EXOTICA SNUGGER FIT CONDOM
1 GOLD CIRCLE COIN CONDOM
1 KIMONO PLUS CONDOM
1 MAXX CONDOM
1 PLEASURE PLUS CONDOM
1 ROUGH RIDER CONDOM
1 SHEIK MINT FLAVORED CONDOM
1 MIDNIGHT DESIRE CONDOM
ASTROGLIDE LUBRICANT SAMPLER
WET PERSONAL LUBRICANT SAMPLER
FORPLAY SENSUAL LUBRICANT SAMPLER
AQUA LUBE LUBRICANT SAMPLER
10 LATEX FINGER COTS
4 LATEX DAMS
4 FINGER TOWELETTES
2 PAIR LATEX GLOVES
1 DICK N'JANE CONDOM
1 LOLLIPOP CONDOM

CONDOMANIA, America's first condom store, introduces its revolutionary safer sex kit. This kit makes a fun and useful introduction into the world of safer sex. At the heart of the kit is a comprehensive safer sex manual which uses hip and honest language to educate and help people negotiate the many issues af safer sex, such as what to do when your partner refuses to practice safer sex.

$19.95

SAFER SEX KIT

TO ORDER CALL 1-800-9CONDOM

A percentage of the sales from CONDOMania's Safer Sex Kit will be donated to two leading organizations which are committed to developing innovative ways to educate people and combat the spread of HIV/AIDS: AIDS Project Los Angeles and Mount Sinai Hospital HIV/AIDS Prevention and Treatment Program, New York.

If you can read this, you're lucky.

Millions of Amercans can't.

Help make America a better place
in which to live, work, and play.

Support your local
literacy volunteer program
by donating your time or money
to help someone learn how to read.

Reading.
We're all for it!

A public service message provided by THREE CAT PRESS.
© 1994 by THREE MOON MEDIA, Inc.

Sensual Products

**How to order them without embarrassment.
How to use them without disappointment.**

Today, people are interested in improving the quality of their lives and exploring their own sensuality with options from the **Xandria Collection**.

The most important aspect of satisfaction is trust. Trust us to make sure that thoughtful consideration goes into choosing each product in the catalogue as to its quality, value, and sensual appeal.

What is The Xandria Collection?

It is a very special collection of sensual products. It includes the finest and most effective products available from around the world. Products that can open new doors to pleasure (perhaps many you never knew existed)!

Our products range from the simple to the delightfully complex. They are designed for the timid, the bold, or for anyone who has ever wished there could be something more to their sensual pleasures.

The Xandria Collection has a unique three-way guarantee. We've had the same, no worry guarantee for nearly 20 years.

First, we guarantee your privacy.

Everything we ship is plainly packaged and securely wrapped, with no clue to its contents from the outside. All transactions are strictly confidential and we <u>never</u> sell, rent or trade any customer's name.

Second, we guarantee your satisfaction.

If a product seems unsatisfactory, simply return it within 60 days for a replacement or refund.

Third, we guarantee the quality of our products for one year.

If it malfunctions, simply return it to us for a replacement.

The Xandria Gold Collection is a tribute to closeness and communication. Celebrate the possibilities for pleasure you each have within. If you're prepared to intensify your own pleasure, then send for the **Xandria Gold Edition Catalogue**. It is priced at just $4.00, which is applied in full to your first order.

Write today. You have absolutely nothing to lose, and an entirely new world of enjoyment to gain.

Did you know that
THREE MOON MEDIA
does more than book publishing?

We also provide
a variety of expert
media production services,
including copywriting, layout,
graphic design, photography
and illustration.

Call us
and we'll tell you
about our high quality,
cost-conscious work
that's always pleasing
to the eye, ear,
and the accoutntant.

THREE MOON MEDIA™
Down To Earth Information For The Imformation Age™
• Technical Manuals • Employee Manuals • Presentations •
• Brochures • Annual Reports • Marketing Materials •
• Print • Audio • Video • CD-ROM • Multimedia •

Telephone:
(305) 867-1060 / (800) BOOKS-101

ACKNOWLEDGMENTS

A heartfelt thanks goes out to all who have made this book a success. To Beth, Reneé, and Matt, thanks for the never-ending flow of creative ideas, encouragement, and hard work; to my mother, Ruth, and my brother, Ira, I will never be able to repay all the love and kindness you have shown me and shown me how to give; to Barbara Pacquin, thanks for being such a good friend; to Susan Lucke and Woody Hollis, your considerate and careful reading was a godsend; to Gayle Coleman of Atlas, Pearlman, Trop & Borkson, thanks for all your expert legal advice, patience, and encouragement; to Mary Gerbic, thanks for your care and diligence; and finally, to my father, Murray, and my grandmother, Lily, your spirit is always with me; rest in peace.

Tannis, I love you.

Shoes shined,

David Abels

THE LEAD PLAYERS

BETH ADELMAN is Editor-in-Chief of THREE CAT PRESS and the editor of *Do It With Your Shoes On & 101 Other Fun Ways To Spice Up Your Sex Life.* A poet and professional magazine editor, Ms. Adelman lives in Brooklyn, New York, with her two cats, Yin and Yang.

RENEE BUNDI designed *Do It With Your Shoes On & 101 Other Fun Ways To Spice Up Your Sex Life.* Ms. Bundi, a magazine art director, graphic designer, and Macintosh expert, lives on Long Island, New York with her cat, Taylor.

MATT SCOTT, a freelance artist and animation student, illustrated *Do It With Your Shoes On & 101 Other Fun Ways To Spice Up Your* Sex Life. Mr. Scott lives with his wife in Columbus, Ohio.

UPCOMING BOOKS & VIDEOS
From THREE MOON MEDIA

from THREE CAT PRESS

No More 9 To 5
Home Office Guerrilla
The Home Office Companion
The Buck Stops Here

from ALTON'S TRAVEL GUIDES

Alton's Honeymoon Havens: New England
Alton's Honeymoon Havens: The Southeast
Alton's Honeymoon Havens: England & France
Alton's Honeymoon Havens: Italy
Alton's Honeymoon Havens: Canada
Alton's Top Student Vacation Spots: Europe

(Videos available for all ALTON'S TRAVEL GUIDE titles)

LET 'EM KNOW YOU MEAN BUSINESS!!!
TELL 'EM TO DO IT WITH THEIR SHOES ON!!!

This beautiful 100% cotton white designer T-shirt comes in five adult men's sizes: S (32-34), M (36-38), L(40-42), XL (44-46), and XX (48 & up; great for night shirts). At $9.95 each, they make great gifts for lovers or for friends. Buy 3 or more and shipping and handling is FREE!!!

(clip here)

- -

(Indicate quantity in appropriate box)

SIZE	S	M	L	XL	XX	TOL
QUANT.						

(1) # of shirts_____ @ $9.95 each   _____

(2) AZ, CA, CO, FL, GA, IL, MA, MN, MO
     NC, NV, PA, TX, VA, and DC residents
     add state and local sales tax on merchandise   _____

(3) Shipping & handling @ $2.50 each
     (on orders of 2 or less)   _____

(4) CA, CO, FL, GA, NC, NY, and TX residents
     add state and local sales on shipping & handling   _____

(5)   **TOTAL**   _____

Make payment payable to:
THREE MOON MEDIA, Inc.
P.O. Box 415106
Miami Beach, FL 33141-5106
TEL: (305)867-1060/(800) BOOKS-101
(Send check or money order please. Do not send cash. Canadian orders must be in U.S. funds.)

Name: _____

Address: _____

City, State, Zip: _____

Tel: (optional, but incase we have question about your order) (_____) _____

BONUS: If you include a "Fun Way To Do It" we haven't mentioned in this book with your order, we'll enter you in our "Spice Up Your Sex Life" contest. The 10 most creative entries will receive a set of five (5) T-shirts FREE!!!
MY FUN WAY TO DO IT:

_____

ABOUT THE AUTHOR

DAVID ABELS is Publisher of THREE CAT PRESS and President of THREE MOON MEDIA, Inc., a media publishing and consulting firm. A member of the National Writers Union and a longtime freelance and staff writer, Mr. Abels holds a B.A. in Accounting & Information Systems and an M.A. in Journalism. He lives with his wife and their three cats in Miami Beach, Florida, and may be contacted at the following address or phone numbers:

THREE CAT PRESS
Post Office Box 415106
Miami Beach, FL 33141-5106
Tel: (305) 867-1060 / (800) BOOKS-101

ABOUT THIS BOOK

Do It With Your Shoes On & 101 Other Fun Ways To Spice Up Your Sex Life will give you and your lover 102 different and exciting ways to pep up your love life. From doing it in sexy underwear to doing it in someone else's house, the tips in this book will provide even the longest of long-term couples the inspiration to get back on the road to orgasmic bliss. Written in a lighthearted but motivational style and packed with hundreds of fun suggestions, *Do It With Your Shoes On & 101 Other Fun Ways To Spice Up Your Sex Life* is sure to put the fire back in your bedroom routine. If your love life has been reduced to an hour of TV and a kiss goodnight before going to bed, get ready, get set, and get going to the sex life you desire, and do it with your shoes on!